HEALING
STORYTELLING

The Art of Imagination and
Storymaking for Personal Growth

Nancy Mellon

Endorsements

Once in a while if you are very lucky you come across a book that stops you in your tracks. As a spontaneous storyteller for some 30+ years I rarely come across a book of such immediacy and engagement for the complete beginner as much as the professional storyteller. It is a 'how-to' storytelling classic. You can open this book anywhere to become fascinated by its content and the incredibly useful storytelling exercises that populate its pages.

— **Alexander MacKenzie**: storyteller in executive education, OSHR Management Consultant, author of an illustrated Hospice book, *Humbert Bear Likes to Doze: Joy in the Face of Adversity.*

Healing Storytelling *portrays adults and children finding healing and creative courage in the midst of even the direst of life stresses. Many teachers, students, community leaders, parents, therapists and other professionals have carried this inspirational book with them, dog-eared and worn, in backpacks and purses, to help them to meet daily challenges.*

— **Robert Smyth**: Yellow Moon Press, Cambridge, Massachusetts, USA

This storytelling classic is packed full of gentle wisdom and inspiration to help develop the imagination. Its focus on the power of storytelling to nourish and sustain us all through hard times is particularly moving and relevant today.

— **Sue Hollingsworth**: storyteller and co-author of *The Storyteller's Way.*

This is one of the most beautiful books written about the power of storytelling to heal body, mind and earth. It is a precious medicine chest of inspiring, profound activity. We need Healing Storytelling.

— **Laura Simms**: storyteller, author of *Our Secret Territory: The Essence of Storytelling and The Robe of Love: Instructions for the Heart.*

Finding the sources to fairy tales, myths and tellings in the form of living images from our inner world is worth gold to budding and seasoned storytellers alike. This is a book to restore our innate intelligence and creativity in wise and delightful ways.

– **Inger Lise Oelrich**: adult educator, storyteller, founder of Nordic Healing Story Alliance and author of *The New Story: Storytelling as a Pathway to Peace*.

This is a handbook for turning straw into gold. I refer to it professionally, and recommend it in every workshop I run training therapists, teachers and parents in storytelling. I turned once again to the wisdom of Nancy Mellon's insights and exercises recently in Singapore, training professionals in prisons, early years settings, mainstream and special schools. During a difficult time, one of her exercises also helped me to bridge a deeply painful personal situation.

– **Louise Coigley**: Speech and Language Pathologist and Therapist, Creator of *Lis'n Tell: Live Inclusive Storytelling*.

Nancy Mellon describes stories as maps to learning and healing. She leads readers into the imaginative and transforming world of traditional story with vast knowledge of their wise symbolic potency. Therapists, teachers, storytellers, and story enquirers everywhere should read this important book, and add it to their library.

– **Mary Smail**: dramatherapist and psychotherapist, SoulWorks, UK.

Sometimes the Wonder Tale of who we are touches in to the everyday happenings of our lives. The exercises in this book show ways to find peace and healing through a conscious engagement with that wise aspect of us which knows and cares for our true story.

– **Paul Matthews**: poet, educator, author of *Sing Me the Creation: Creative Writing Sourcebook* and *Words in Place*.

Healing Storytelling was first published as *Storytelling and the Art of the Imagination* in 1992 by Element Books, USA and as *The Art of Storytelling* by Element Books, Australia in a second edition. It was then published by Yellow Moon Press, Cambridge, MA, USA from 2003 to 2018, as *Storytelling and the Art of Imagination*, ISBN: 978-0-938756-66-8.

Hawthorn Press gratefully acknowledges the help of Robert Smyth of Yellow Moon Press with this new, third updated edition.

Cover image © Arthur Penn
Cover design by Lucy Guenot
Typesetting in Scala by Winslade Graphics
Reprinted 2022 by CMP (UK) Ltd, Dorset

British Library Cataloguing in Publication Data applied for
ISBN: 978-1-912480-13-5
eISBN: 978-1-912480-21-0

HEALING
STORYTELLING

The Art of Imagination and
Storymaking for Personal Growth

Nancy Mellon

Hawthorn Press

CONTENTS

Dedication

*This book is dedicated with loving gratitude
to the late Adam and Gisela Bittleston, to my
family, and to the many individuals and families
I have met along my journey who have helped me
to find my way. I am deeply indebted to many
inspiring people who are connected with the
international Waldorf School Movement.*

Foreword

For thousands of years, story making and storytelling have been integral to our humanity. More than a source of entertainment, stories in every culture have taught moral and history lessons to adults and children alike, and kept complex traditions alive. Through story language we have learnt about the mountains and the forests, the earth and the sea, the stars and the moon, and those who came before us. It is often through storytelling and the art of the imagination that fears have been faced, and hurdles overcome.

Meeting challenges, big and small, by tapping into imaginative narrative is natural and unique to us as a human species. Yet as Nancy Mellon points out in her introduction to this book, our modern imaginations are often broken, warped and fearful.

Especially now in our modern fast-paced age, so obsessively dominated by the internet and other virtual experiences, we need stories to help us to create authentic relationships with ourselves and one another. This book offers a feast of ideas that inspires the reader to slow down and develop healthy imaginations and wholesome real-life story interactions. A manual for personal and group creativity, it is a wonderful healing resource.

Stories can soothe our souls, and touch our hearts. They can change our perspectives, motivate and strengthen us on many levels as they bridge unseen and visible worlds and connect us to all life. Indigenous communities worldwide hold a deep respect for their sacred healing capacity.

Nancy details a rich supply of examples from her healing work with both adults and children. The author insists that every human being is born a storyteller, and that our troubles are fuel for genuine transformations to occur. She shares how imaginative story making has helped multitudes of others, as well as herself, to transform personal challenges.

An anecdote the author shares that speaks deeply to me is a story she wrote one spring morning called The Flower Hater. Her mother did not want flowers in the house because they reminded her of her mother's funeral when she was a child. Nancy, now an avid gardener, was able to lift away a shadow that had been hovering all her life. She states, 'Writing the story was like a healing dream. I was liberated through respecting the truth of my imagination.'

Many more such intimate sharings from Nancy's life and the lives of her students of all ages are woven into the pages of every chapter. All were eager to experiment with the healing power of story making. My own imagination has been deliciously nourished by reading the range of inspirational anecdotes and exercises in this book that can be applied with courageous intention as healing salves to a multitude of ills.

Stories are as important to our soul life as water is to our well-being. They can revive, and rejuvenate; they are vital for healthy growth and development; they find their way into our hearts, and our very being. This book is a shining wellspring for readers to dip into, and continue on their journey, enlivened and refreshed. Whatever your walk of life, it offers invaluable guidance and encouragement for your creativity to thrive, perhaps in ways you have never before imagined.

As a therapeutic storyteller, I know from personal experience with teachers, therapists and parents who have attended my seminars in many different countries, people everywhere are thirsting for healing imagination. Many years ago Nancy helped my first book come into being, and in 2008 she generously penned its foreword. Now life has come full circle and the honour is mine. I am sure you will enjoy this inspirational guidebook to healing imagination, in many ways, and on many levels.

Susan Perrow
Therapeutic storyteller, teacher trainer, parent educator and counsellor

Introduction

This is a book to help restore story wisdom to your daily life. A treasure-trove of imaginative powers lives within us all. These powers often lie stunned and dormant, yet to awaken the pictures that live in our story-imagination is to become more fully and radiantly alive. Although setbacks of all kinds may discourage us, the grand, old process of storytelling puts us in touch with strengths we may have forgotten, with wisdom that has faded or disappeared, and with hopes that have fallen into darkness. It also connects us to joys and pleasures that have been relegated to professional entertainers. Above all, storytelling gives us love and courage for life: in the process of making up a wonderful story, new spirit is born for facing the great adventures of our lives and for giving wise encouragement to others, of any age, along their own path ways. Every storyteller collects and arranges vital inner pictures; behind these live universal ordering principles. I offer this book as a way for you to tap into these life-giving patterns. It is meant to be used as a companion to the story collections that you may know or have yet to discover, some of which are listed at the back of this book.

Reading wonderful stories from the past empowers you to speak and to write your own stories. To make up and tell an original story, however, is quite a different experience than reading or reciting stories already formulated in books or on screens. For several years I have had the privilege of working with parents, prospective parents, teachers, librarians, and people in the healing professions. Together we have brought to life the art of storytelling for our selves, for the children in our lives, and for each other. My purpose, whether exploring old stories or helping to create new ones during storytelling courses and workshops that I have held, has been to enliven speaking, and to awaken the lifegiving and transformative energies that help us through our difficulties. Every detail in a story, its characters, landscape, moods, and the meanderings of plot can be circulated through our own bodies, feelings, and the structures of our minds. If we experience the reality of each part of the story as an aspect of ourselves, no matter how grand or dilapidated, or fantastical it may be, it will be an enlivening experience. As we bring adult awareness to everything that happens and everyone in our stories, we grow accordingly in our sense of who we are and in our relationships with all kinds of people and happenings.

What is active healthy imagination? My experience with adults and children has shown me that our twenty-first century imaginations often are broken, fearful, warped, obsessive; yet given guidance, inspiration, and encouragement, they can become, even quite suddenly, wholesome and radiant. Steadied by wise old elements of the imaginative world, we can surge and play with the rich energies of its themes and images, as dreamers and poets do. Powerful old story themes, language, and imagery moving through our psyches act like good food, causing the body and blood to rise up with joy and eager breathing. The process of storytelling itself, through voice, gesture, and goodwill and through the fonts of wisdom it opens, evokes from deep within a healthy state of creative adventure.

This book is intended to meet different kinds of needs. Each of its short, evocative essays and the examples that accompany them are gentle tickles to encourage you – perhaps despite yourself – to go forward in joy and wonder toward a life full of love and the wise use of power. It is first of all intended as a guidebook to those inner gestures, energies, landscapes, and characters that awaken from time to time from the deep springs of imagination. It is a book for anyone at home by the fireside and bedside, in schools, and in therapeutic settings who is seeking a more self-aware, meaningful, and positive relationship to the sometimes overpowering and confusing world of imagination. It will help you to better delineate and experience that world in a personal and positive way.

This book is not arranged to teach specific story plots; many resources already exist that share the grand old stories – summarizing, analyzing, and interpreting them for us from different points of view. The method here is to touch, page by page, upon the pulse points of various grand old tales in order to enliven similar creative pulse-points in the reader. Consequently, more personal integrity may be experienced during the reading, telling, and creating process. Most of the stories and myths that are mentioned come from European sources, yet their themes are common to many languages and countries, having been filtered through the genius of the time and the folk who lived there.

The ultimate purpose of this book is to foster the creation of fresh, healthy, new stories to help us better meet the challenges of our times. Healthy and helpful stories spontaneously well from us wherever we are, whenever we are willing to let them. To make a wholesome, spirited story that truly meets the moment is a process that enlivens us from deep within, arousing a sense of wonder and joy to strengthen us on our sometimes overwhelming and bewildering journeys.

When I began my career, teaching a variety of subjects at different locations, I thought how happy I would be as a traveling storyteller. Then everything could be wrapped up joyfully into one role. But in those days storytelling did not have the enthusiastic appreciation it formerly had in America. Besides, I was shy and withdrawn. For a number of years instead of storytelling, I stood before classes of children and young adults and, for the most part, shared books and the ways of language with them.

One day I had a great surprise. I was asked to keep a feisty class of children busy for an hour because their teacher was ill. How was I to keep them quiet? I had just enough time to search out something to read to them; since it was Saint Patrick's Day, I chose some tales collected by W. B. Yeats, the Irish poet. I opened my mouth to read and out came an authentic Irish accent that astonished me. I kept on reading; the children were as entranced as I was listening to the story I had selected and to my voice. The words sang through me. My heart had opened wide. At the end of the hour, I closed the book and my Irish voice was gone. That experience served as a great opening for me. I wondered how many cultural roots were living at the base of my tongue, waiting to emerge in story-song.

In the years that followed, as I learned to hear myself, I could listen more and more deeply to the quiescent voices in the children and adults from many lands and cultures who entered my classrooms. I loved helping them to free themselves into poetry and stories and into declamations in debate. Tell us your dream! Tell us your memories!

Describe who you love and the taste of truth!

At long last I discovered Waldorf Education, and this was my true entry into an old cause. To tell a great story well, I learned in my education classes as I prepared to teach in a Waldorf School, is my duty. Not to know the story as part of my mental collection but to feel it, as the liveliest child might, all the way down to my toes. Not to think of imagination as a historical activity but as daily necessity. Soon I would have to make up and to tell stories every day to maintain the high standards of the best of Waldorf School teachers. According to this creative method, I began to strengthen and to regulate my own sporadic imagination in new ways to meet the needs of the children that I was teaching. I began to believe in earnest that storytellers have as profound a purpose as any who are charged to guide and transform human lives. I knew it as an ancient discipline and vocation to which everyone is called.

One day, in the course of my training as a Waldorf teacher in England, I encountered one of several people who have greatly changed my life. Gisela Bittleston was to become my puppetry teacher and the teacher of my soul. I met her for the first time within a glowing little jewel of a theater speaking and singing in high vibrato a Rumanian puppet play, 'The White Wolf'. The beautiful story was about an enchanted white wolf whose gentle lover had to journey to the farthest stars to find the light to transform him into the true prince that he was. This was a story about the total determination of the human spirit for self-transformation. The universal theme at that moment deeply touched my soul.

Thus began my relationship with fairy tales, for as a child, like many of my generation, I had only slight interest and pleasure in fairy tales. Today I often enjoy telling people how un-American I had believed storybook princes and princesses to be. I understand very well the resistance we can have to the kinds of characters and landscapes that are invoked in this book. Yet in many subsequent puppet productions, as my right hand, my left hand, and my voice portrayed characters that my 'democratic' skeptical mental attitudes rejected, I took on new life! As I opened myself to splendid, new possibilities in childhood education, I also had begun, with vistas undreamed of, the reeducation of my own 'inner child'. I found a deeper breathing.

My joy at working with the beauty and·truth behind folk and fairy-tale pictures gradually was opening me up to unfamiliar qualitites of mind and heart. My soul was now ranging through archetypal energies, and through many different cultures and moods of soul. As I spoke and sang the tones of a mournful queen, an enchanted prince, a wicked witch, an eager princess, or a powerful shaman, I discovered lost and undeveloped parts of myself. I had become a grateful puppeteer, portraying stories from behind the red curtains of my story theater. I could whimper and cry! I could sing soulfully because the queen longed for a child, or because the beautiful child needed to sing in the story. I could laugh like a horrid witch or wizard, and I could dispel wicked enchantments with one resounding word. I became so enthusiastic that I taught many others to create puppet productions so that they might share this way of feeling into a story and receiving its gifts.

After a time, I discovered that through all the many hours I had spent with stories from around the world – changing the lighting from scene to scene, creating hand puppets and props with many sorts of young and old people, refining the gestures and voices – I had somehow won from these old tales the power to make up new stories. I was no longer a timid soul; I had found immeasurable new breath, understanding, and purpose. I was creating stories for the children I taught, and I was being invited to parties as the storyteller. 'Marcus needs a story for his fifth birthday because he wants so much to fly that we are afraid he will jump off a cliff.' 'Serena wants more than anything to be a prince and seems so bossy and intense. If only she could hear a story about herself.' 'Joseph attacks his sister as if she were an armed guard.' Baffled and inspired again and again into creativity for the children, my old dream was coming true: I was sitting in the midst of families and in classrooms, listening to myself create story medicine.

My way of working with stories today is as a tool for self-transformation. I give prescriptions for self-healing through stories. These days much attention is given to finding and healing our 'inner child'. Age is not a factor in story therapeutics: 'Divine Enfant' and 'Wise Old Sage' live within everyone. The spontaneous wisdom woven into the core of every person is the essence of life. It is this wisdom that we tap into in the storytelling process. It is like prayer; it reassures and strengthens us. Of course, we have to go through whatever resistance we may feel as we return to this core. Is there any pain, sorrow, or nightmare too terrible to be told through a story? Are there fears and bewilderments too deep for a story to hold?

Story makers ultimately accept all earthly feelings and carry them as wise children into the realms of joy. I invite people to reach into my great round basketful of archetypal figures and, with the kind assistance of the puppets, to bring forth the aspirations and dramas of their inner lives. Or, seated around a candle in a circle of care and creativity, to write and to share spontaneously a tale from their own wise imaginations. Or, to sit apart in pairs for a while and tell stories to one another as if their lives depended on it.

Because I myself resisted becoming a storyteller, I appreciate the powers that are stored within you, though perhaps entirely hidden, which can flourish with affirmation and guidance. When it is time for a story, I say to myself and to others: Take a good deep breath, plunge in and keep swimming; the waters will keep us up. Or dance, fly. Or jump into the volcano. In the realm of stories, all will be made well.

Beginning and Ending

Sey forth thy tale, and tarry not
the time. – Geoffrey Chaucer

A STORY FIRE

The campfire and hearth, around which people of all ages have gathered for comfort and warmth under the slow movements of the sun, moon, and stars, is a picture of our inner selves. We have a place of warmth and light within us. Around this centering place, feelings, pictures, and words gather. As we hold ourselves steadily to this inner flame, all that moves toward its healing light, whether experienced as friend or foe, will be warmed and illuminated.

You, like every human being, are a storyteller by birthright. You are born with an endless supply of personal and universal themes. It is important to open yourself to receive the vast wealth of imagery that lives within you. Build a hearth within you and let it become a circle of protection. In it your heart's wisdom may ignite and burn. Ask that all who gather at your fire from your own inner skies, lands, and waters come with goodwill to share their truths in its warmth. May whoever comes to listen receive openly what is created within the safe boundaries of your story world.

Before I begin any storytelling session, even during daylight hours, I light a candle. You might wish to use votive candles in a clear or colored glass since they provide a glow from within. Sometimes choosing the right candle color will strengthen a mood, such as green for freshness, pink for loving gentleness, red for courage. You might light candles for the main characters in a story. At Christmas time one year, I was invited to tell a birthday story to a room full of parents with babies and toddlers. This time I sang softly as I lit a row of little white candles set into the branch of a silver birch tree. The children remained content throughout the story, their eyes on the seven little flames.

Once I visited a house that was ideal for family storytelling. It had an open hearth at its center. The foot of the master bed came close to it on one side, the living room couch on the other; moveable curtains opened up the whole house. The mother of the house, who was its architect, always wanted to feel the hearth at the center of her home. Whatever space is chosen for stories, everyone who listens well helps to create the story.

Sit in silence before a living flame. Think carefully of the fire's story: the long years of weather that nourished the tree in the hearth; the wide-ranging flights of the bees that made the candle's wax; the tiny spark that brought it to its present illumination. Let the story of the outer fire gradually lead you inward to feel the story of the light and warmth that you carry within you.

BREATHING NEW LIFE

Beginnings are like births – they have emptiness and openness. They offer a place of warm receptivity into which the new child can safely arrive. The silent period before the story is a very sacred time. It links you and your listeners with the creative power of the universe. Time and the breath change. It is a moment to call out wisdom and let it stream naturally from the earth and the heavens toward you. Our breath helps us move beyond the barriers of mere reasoning and clock time. It takes us past any blocking fears and resistances into the redeeming powers of the imagination. Breathe in the silence before you say anything. As your familiar outer life closes, inner vision will open. Feel a listening space within your heart, and expectancy in your limbs and belly. Your story is a gestating 'child' of the universe. This will help you to know how to receive that which will now unfold according to its own laws. Some stories do abort, but they may return stronger at a later time with all their life-forces intact and in good order. You will act as midwife and husband to your own story, helping it to come forth and be known.

As you prepare yourself to tell a story, you might play on a simple flute or recorder, or strum a lyre or other stringed instrument. Chimes, a bell, or singing also clear the air. Simple musical patterns help to bring about a sense of vibrant expectation. As you tune the air, you also clear the space within which the story is beginning to resonate. The more alive and fresh the atmosphere you create within and around you, the more vital your story images and word-music will be.

A friend of mine, who is a storyteller, has made her home on a rise of what was once American Indian land. She has filled her living room there with an astonishing collection of musical instruments. She chooses the appropriate instrument for each story she tells; sometimes she uses several instruments for one story. Though she complains that she never practices enough, her listeners take much pleasure in the blending of her voice with their sounds, and the comforting sight of the instruments in her lap and around where she sits. Thea has chronic, serious asthma, yet playing, singing, and telling stories has given her many thousands of hours of healthy breathing. You, too, can clear away whatever obstructions there may be to your voice and breath as you immerse yourself in storytelling.

Hum and breathe. Whistle and then breathe in slowly. Sing a clear tone and then sit in silence listening to the air around your head, which has now been changed.

Organize a place in your home, whether it be one shelf or a whole room, that you can devote to your collection of storytelling activities, books, and musical instruments.

ADVENTURERS

At the beginning of any story, you will have to describe a protagonist or two. Whether feminine or masculine, young or old, human or otherwise, central characters carry qualities of youthful exuberance and trust. They set out, however reluctantly, together or alone, toward a wider horizon. The energy of your story will create pictures to move your main characters beyond the protection of the 'father's castle' and the boundaries of the 'mother's hearth' – a deep breath that leads us out into a new, strange, and larger sense of who we are. Beyond the breath of 'once upon a time' and 'long ago and far away' is the breath that invites us to launch out into the mysteries of human identity. Protagonists may take many forms and guises; but, whether they are royal or humble, reluctant or determined, strong or handicapped, male or female, animal, human, or divine, their exuberant spirit of adventure awakens our own.

Invite your storyteller to affirm you as you are at this moment and to introduce you further to who you are. The identity of all your story characters, however strange, weird, or powerful they may be, are safely known to your highest self. Your story will gather momentum as you acknowledge that you are part of the whole flow of the earth's evolution and that your story characters are guided and cared for just as you, in the mysteries of your destiny, are guided and cared for by a wisdom greater than your own.

When I am privileged to act as midwife to people's stories, I usually ask them to sit together in pairs or three together. Sometimes when people are beginning to explore storytelling as a way of knowing themselves and others better, I first give them a wise old tale to read aloud to one another or a selection of puppets to hold as I read to them. They are soon ready to begin their own spontaneous stories. A woman who was overcoming a serious illness and had suffered an abusive childhood recently took the time to write about her experiences:

I do not know how to communicate the richness I find in storytelling. The first day I started crying as you gave the instructions and then a story just poured out of me; I was absolutely amazed. I never liked fairy tales, never read them. I could barely read the script the week before. Yet telling the story was something completely different. I knew it was the story of my life. In four minutes I had captured the spirit of my whole life as it felt to me at that moment.

After telling this story there was a change in me that allowed me to trust my own boundaries, and I gave M. the keys to my house. The shift happened very rapidly. It was not at a conscious level. Each story led to a similar change. When I tell a story, I speak from my heart. I start out with trust, and I listen as the story pours out of me. When I become stuck, I wait or sometimes express consternation through the character if that is appropriate. I am very careful not to judge but to let the story be revealed to me. These stories come from a place inside of me which I know no other way to tap.

Think of exhilarating moments in your life when you overcame hesitation and fear and went forward on an adventure. This is the mood to invoke when you begin a story.

In two or three minutes, spontaneously create a story character or two. Whether you speak aloud or write down your description, be sure not to cramp yourself with self judgments and analysis. Storytelling is an exhilarating adventure.

NAMING

As a storyteller, you may exercise vast freedom in the realm of names. Like parents who find names for the children who come their way, sometimes adding to their formal names special endearments, storytellers can reach out into the whole universe of sounds to find names for characters and for the places that they inhabit. Angels may be depicted bringing names to parents and guardians. Names may be found in dreams or written on water or stone. Even the most 'ordinary' names may carry within them secrets and be spoken with a deep and tender sense of awe. The sound of 'ah' in a name creates a sense of opening: Ananda, Ali Baba, Alyosha, Fatima, Hans, Bambino. The brave sound of 'o' invokes total inclusiveness: ocean, home, lone prairie. 'Oo' brings a sense of intense wonder with perhaps some fear mixed in. The sound of 'ee' in a name suggests a character with a strong sense of identity. A playful, light-hearted character will need a name of similar playfulness built of quick little syllables. A wilful and intense character will need strong consonants, such as 'k', 't', 'j', and 'f.' A gentle one will attract sounds that are soft and flowing: 'b', 'n', 'm', and 'l'.

The process of building up names that are sensitive to the characteristics of a particular person and place is a natural one. Books of names, with long lists of evocative ones from many parts of the world, are available for purchase and in libraries. The index of a world atlas will give new ideas for place names. Book sources encourage us into greater confidence and awareness of our birthright: to name, and to know through names, who and where we are in ourselves and in relationship to others. It is only to human beings that this ability to discover and to remember names has been given.

You are one with the universe of sounds; you can listen for their vibrations within you. Names breathe through the light of day and in the darkness of starry nights. They emanate from all things and beings. As a storyteller, you have great opportunities to discover them as you inhabit your imaginary spaces. All names and names never before spoken are within your grasp as you create your stories.

When a group has gathered together to explore storytelling, I often invite them to introduce themselves not through their usual name but through a name that they make up. To find a fresh and loving name for oneself is an interesting experience. Many long to be known by another name yet have not had an opportunity or sufficient motivation to change the one they were born with. These names and the ones that people create in stories often amaze us all. They flow out so naturally: *Sidera*, *Desertina*, and *Shehan* are three I have heard recently that seem to capture the essence of a character.

Listen very deeply into your heart and soul and come up with a new name or set of names for yourself. Perhaps you would also like to find a fresh and sonorous name for other people who are important to you.

Create a name for the kingdom of your heart's desire, a place where your deepest longings may be fulfilled. Find a name for the place where you can leave all the unwanted 'baggage' in your heart and mind.

VOICES

Stored within you and everyone is a capacity for speaking the truths of wind, rock, flower, and cloud – of all earth's creatures and for articulating the truth of human beings of every sort. To do this, we need only to open and develop our listening capacity.

Physical ears are the curling outer shells for our whole capacity to listen. In stories of many lands, characters sometimes receive, through magical means, the ability to listen and to understand the voices of birds, animals, and wind more than usual. They may even be enabled to listen into the radiance of the sun, moon, and stars and receive clear messages and guidance from them.

Stories like these remind us that intimate meaning inheres in every living thing and that the whole world speaks, if only we can listen and comprehend. Within the safe boundaries of a story, a character whose power of listening is greatly expanded helps us to awaken to the potentialities of our own hearing. The callouses built up of necessity against the din of our daily encounters with modern civilization can be softened, at least for a time. As our sense of hearing expands, all our other senses tend to expand with it, including our sense of self and our relationship with the universe.

As you let yourself open up to each resounding moment of your story, stones, trees, and insects that live and journey through the landscapes of your imagination can speak of themselves. Stones can chant their rhythmic purpose on earth. Plants can sing and call with clear voices into your story world. Animals can speak their needs and offer their assistance. Winds can intone from the depths of the seasons. What cannot sing and speak through stories? In these days of shriveling powers of speech and dulled hearing, it is important to create new and deeper powers of listening within yourself and your characters.

Some people open up to imagination primarily through their sense of hearing; others through seeing, movement, or touch; the sense of taste and of smell are also doors to the inner life. Recently I was privileged to suddenly hear the singing of a woman in her fifties; she had been spontaneously creating a story with two others. At first her beautiful song was almost inaudible, yet the words and the melody were flowing from her lips in a pure stream. She kept on singing quietly with all her heart. The man sitting opposite her was tenderly holding a doll he had named D. E. He told us this stood for Divine Enfant, but he said the baby was being brought up by a 'wired mother' who lacked feeling for his/her real needs. The child awakened her compassion. At the end of our time together, I asked her to remember her song. She looked at me doubtfully and sadly. I said, 'Remember it for all the hurt children. You can sing it for the rest of your life.' Then she smiled radiantly. Later she said that she had stood barefoot in a stream with the man she loved most dearly and had sung freely for a long time.

Depths of imagination open depths of sound and of language. I have often been amazed and awed at the beautiful words and syntax that can flow from children who, in their ordinary speech, can sound guttural and monosyllabic. A ten-year-old chatterbox was in one of my story drama groups, slouching and gossiping, her eyes staring emptily. I wondered if she would be able to join in with the others. As we began, I said with more conviction than usual: 'Now your ordinary voices can rest and your storytelling voices can come forth. You can let your voice be beautiful.' In her story, she became a princess with exquisite and natural courtesy who commanded the respect of her mother, the queen. In her story of royal compassion, she rested eloquently from the hysterical chattering, which she had learned from her real mother. Her back straightened and her eyes cleared. When the story was over, the whole group and I knew about the true princess who lived quietly within her.

Opening our speech center is one of the most powerful things we can do for ourselves and for others. Books on 'toning' and on speech formation are shining additions to any library.

Make up a little song, with a very simple melody, about someone or something you love. Whatever you may 'think' of yourself, sing it at least seven times until it becomes a little chant. Accept your child-self that enjoys word repetition, and the feeling of being surrounded by its own loving sounds.

Tell a story in which human beings have lost the power of speech and of singing. Have the protagonist(s) go in search of these powers, being helped by the sun, moon, wind, water, and a number of compassionate creatures.

BEGINNINGS

In the realms of true imagination you can rise up to full height, strength, and vitality. The complexities of daily life – work, enjoyment, and rest – sometimes can seem shriveling, even dead ends. In the story world, a sense of movement toward fulfilment and redemption predominates. When this positive momentum seems lost, leaving you feeling drawn down into many reductions of your life-power, the 'once upon a time' mood, which most grand old tales possess, allows you to experience for yourself fresh entry into time. 'Once' brings a sense of immediacy; 'upon' lifts the storyscape up into imagination; 'a time' takes you and your listeners both forward and backward, until you arrive at a point of creative stillness from which the happenings of the story can creatively unfold. You have the power to bring to birth a story that refreshes time, space, and your sense of life and of who you are. As a storyteller, you are a co-creator with the thriving life of the universe. When I work with people privately and in small groups, I give simple, positive suggestions. I know that everyone has joined the group to challenge themselves. If anyone hesitates for long to begin a story, I say,

> Your breath will propel you along, wherever you are in your story. If you think you can't begin, that is an especially precious moment. You feel the greatest resistance when you are on the verge of greatest discovery. Breathe! Begin, go on, and keep going on to the end!

Soon the air is alive with fresh beginnings and an air of expectancy and creative enjoyment. There are giggles and laughter – bemusement and often tears well up or flow down. Speaking with loving imagination from our core brings with it a sense of release. The spontaneous child-self, whose soul is naturally eloquent, sometimes has been confined for many years. I rarely work with anyone who does not cry sometime during story explorations. I honor these tears. Sorrow usually leads to great smiles of contentment eventually, even uproarious laughter – and to tears of joy.

Before I discovered myself through storytelling, I had been an emotional stoic for many years, with few feelings to call my own. Now I have a handkerchief collection in different styles and colors, which I keep in a handmade basket where people gather in my home. 'Joy and Woe are woven fine', wrote the great English poet, William Blake. As I wash and iron these handkerchiefs, I am reminded of the different tears that have touched them. Sometimes I ask people to keep their tissues in a special place for a while, if they have not cried for a long time, to remember and to honor the welling of their feelings. The ones most repelled by this idea at first can be the most grateful later.

Read aloud the words that begin six or seven wise, old tales, perhaps from one of the story collections listed at the back of this book. Choose one of these beginnings as the starting place for your own story. Here are some examples:

There once lived a King's son who had a bride whom he loved very much.

There was once a wonderful musician, who went forlorn through a forest and thought of all manner of things, and when nothing was left for him to think about he said: 'Time is beginning to pass heavily on me here in the forest. I will fetch hither a good companion for myself.'

Once upon a time an old queen who was ill thought to herself, 'I am lying on what must be my deathbed'.

Once there was a girl who did nothing but spin and weave.

ENDINGS

The great majority of wise, old tales end happily. How can you benefit from ending your stories in a positive mood? Hope is food and fuel: Its immaterial nutrients circulate through us from the evolutionary centers of our universe. Wise story makers always have fed from these sources. They were charged with giving out consolation and hope, like holy chanting water and wine at royal gatherings and at humble altars of hearth and village fountain, their inspiration and work being to improve and strengthen the spirit of all their listeners, at whatever stage of their development and belief. Today you can follow the same healing patterns that were written into the hearts and tongues of earlier story makers, who found listeners especially wherever traditional religion had lost its appeal. In the wise old art of storytelling a 'happy ending' is holy. It cleanses old sorrow and rewards all trials and tribulations. 'And they lived happily ever after' is the equivalent of a triumphant finale. It is as if a bud has been released to flower in a joyous dance with the open skies.

An archetypal happy ending binds two themes. The first is true love found and celebrated throughout the land. The second is self rule. When two souls are united, perhaps after great anguish and opposition, our childlike self is deeply satisfied to know that the union is to continue 'forever after', or at least that '... if they have not died they are living still'. At the end of an ordinary fairy tale, if the simpleton or other traveler has become a 'king' or a 'queen' with a great inheritance, this speaks to the part of our selves that, beyond any material possessions, seeks to experience ourselves as abundantly wise rulers in our own realms.

The classic fairy-tale ending gives a golden 'blueprint' for our ultimate growth toward steady, wise rulership; its wedded bliss tells us that we are all one and eternal when we experience true love. We are free to end our lives in tribulation, sorrow, cynical withdrawal, irony, and bitterness. Or, we may strive to rise beyond all these and bring ourselves to a resolute sense of celebration. As a storyteller you have the privilege of feeding again and again from the fonts of wisdom, which also nourish all the world's great religions. You can develop in a special way through deep imprints in your imagination, faith for your crowning tasks on earth.

In the majority of wise, old tales, joyful endings resolve a problem. Sometimes a quandary may be a very deep one. For the three years I have known her, an unusually spiritual person has been writing a series of stories in which two lost, young children are searching for their true King and Queen. Every now and then she shares the latest instalment with me. Recently her story took the children, who had made themselves invisible, into a dark forest. There they found a king and his queen surrounded by many huntsmen. Yet, the children soon discovered them to be dangerous impostors, disguised in the royal robes.

During the three years that this woman has allowed her imagination to take her very lonely 'inner child' on these adventures for her own sake, she has created a number of stories for troubled children; as a school counselor, she has been able to share the stories with them, their classmates, and their families. Soon the school principal where she works was also showing a positive interest in her storytelling, as were a number of enthusiastic and grateful parents.

Select one of the endings below that were created often with great surprise and satisfaction, by people like yourself. Tell a story out of your own imagination that leads to this ending.

And on the rock, hidden underneath the Old Woman's rose bush, a tiny elf sat happily watching the party, one leg crossed over the other.

She came out of the water and lay down in the grass under the dazzling golden light. She noticed all the fruit on the trees and many green birds in the trees. She saw people coming through the meadow. She went out to meet them. They came up to her and took her hands and embraced her.

'I think we have learned much today', he said. They embraced and they danced for a long time between the darkness and the light.

After ridding the castle of cobwebs and bandits, the prince and princess became king and queen of the land. At last rule was restored and I imagine they are living there still.

2

Movement and a Sense of Direction

Lovers don't finally meet somewhere.
They're in each other all the time. – Rumi

STORY MUSIC

As you tell stories, life-powers which may be hidden away within you can recover beat and rhythm. The melodies of many moods can reverberate through your story imagery. You have a sense of coordination that wells up naturally in your muscles and limbs. However constrained and awkward you may feel in your ordinary life, you know deep within you how to move with delightful vitality. Goals and ordering principles will set you off in a story pattern with a great sense of order and purpose as if you are moving within a musical composition. Language will take on beat and tone. Hold off the impulse to spoof, mock, and sentimentalize the wise, old, well-known story forms even a little while, and their rich, healthy vitality will now well up for you from the original source.

You can take pleasure in listening consciously for the inner music of the great old tales, and in forming your own stories with similar thematic flow and counterpoint. Classical fairy tales, like classical symphonies, mark time majestically. The form of 'Little Snow White' in the original Grimm's collection shows us many of the grand elements of story structure. A theme is introduced at the beginning: yearning, birth, and death. When the child is born, the good queen dies. This death resolves the beautiful opening section. The stepmother embodies the counter-theme; her pride turns into envy and murderous jealousy from which the child must be saved. The middle section of the story surrounds the lovely, growing child with the protection of the seven dwarfs, whose nature is full of the strength and hardihood of the mountains in which they live and work. The stepmother's cruelty intrudes into this realm until the harmonies of the seven little workers are almost broken by her power. In the finale, a princely lover arrives to restore her to life, whose potent love shines into the ice of her bondage to the jealous queen, returning her to the human realm with the dwarfs' blessings.

An innocent meets opposition; help comes; then more opposition and more help alternate until the ultimate resolution of love and fulfilment. This basic story rhythm has a deep connection to our human heartbeat, which moves regularly through three expansions and contractions until one complete circulation has been completed. Whether long or short, a story may be experienced as a symphonic word picture circulating through the chambers of a joyously expanding heart. The tempo of a tale may be discovered and controlled by the teller as a piece of music is discovered and interpreted by a musician. A largo telling may create a mood of melancholic catharsis, *allegro moderato*, a sense of sprightly balance. Fast-paced tripling on the tongue – *vivace, molto vivace, or furioso* tales or episodes – appeal to the swift mercurial energies of teller and listener alike. Silences between words and episodes can be as eloquent in a story as in a piece of music. Within the bounds of any tale, several themes and rhythms may hold sway, giving tongue, heart, and mind the satisfaction of a contrapuntal journey through the realms of time.

The musical patterns of the human heart are the foundation for the most powerful and beautiful stories that have been created and told on this earth. As you stay in touch with your pulse and heartbeat, the breath with which you formulate your story-music will be charged with warmth and flowing rhythms. These will propel the story forward naturally. In the midst of telling your story from your heart, you will be in touch with profound principles that live in your story language and in all harmonious forms.

Whatever your favorite instrument, tell a well-known fairy tale entirely through spontaneous musical composition. Afterwards you may wish to write the music down.

Music unlocks images and the power of speech. Ask each person in a storytelling group to bring a favorite musical instrument, or, provide a variety of instruments for them to choose from. Each instrument may represent a character in the story, a story landscape, a place, and/or a 'magic spell'. Ask the group to create a spontaneous story completely through the interaction of the musical instruments. Simple instruments may be used, such as castanets, triangle, and drum, that can interact with whistling, strumming, and/or singing. Ask the group to practice their story until they know it musically by heart, then present it to others. The others may wish to guess what the story is about, or after the musical presentation, someone in the group may want to put the story into words.

To become more aware of your power to regulate the speed and rhythm of your words as a storyteller, tell the same story in a variety of tempos.

Try singing an entire story to yourself, like an uninhibited child in a beautiful garden with only the bees, ants, and trees as your audience. A courageous elderly woman said that she had always explored life with a brace around her neck, which constantly restricted her breathing. In your story, an iron band locked around your story heart or throat may snap.

DESCENDING

As you are creating a story, a sudden or persistent urge to dig down may surprise you. Or, you may feel like falling down, like Alice did, through an already existing tunnel into 'Wonderland'. If you follow this descent, you will come to deeper levels of earth life and of yourself. Downward ardor may lead to exciting, ominous fires and darkness, to caverns in which are hidden gems and jewels of wisdom and power. Guardians of these depths may astonish you with their appearances and behavior. You may meet wild beasts, dragons, and shadow monsters that have lain in wait there with tests, passwords, mirror games, and mysterious hungers, that can be appeased, perhaps, only by magical means.

As you descend into story terrain, you also may discover gnomes and dwarfs, elemental workers in the under-earth. Curdie found them in the mining mountains of Scotland in the story world of George MacDonald. The magnetic brilliance of their jeweled realms constitutes a main theme in the Germanic myths that were dramatized by Richard Wagner in his 'Ring Cycle of the Nibelungenlied' Dungeons in old castles may chain a noble traveler, such as biblical Daniel, who was held captive in the dark for his ability to accurately interpret dreams. Greek and ancient American Indian lore portray a maiden who goes down into the shadowy realms below the surface of the known earth and there meets the spirits of those who have died and are buried. As an adventurer in the under-earth, the maiden is initiated in the ways of the realms of the dead. She becomes a queen, and in her royal role becomes a helper and guide to the souls who, when they are prepared, can receive the touch of her radiant wisdom and return to the realms of light and fresh air. George MacDonald created uniquely feminine and benevolent helpers in the underworld, wearing luminous crowns and gowns and shoes. These powerful feminine presences unfailingly find and help children lost down there. A monk may be praying ceaselessly in a deep cavern, although in and around him burn fires of fabulous hues and intensities.

Courage to descend into story terrain may lead in many directions at once. Similarly, our bodies contain many mysterious caverns, openings, and branching circulations of nerves and blood. A story can illuminate the lower depths of our circulatory powers. These connect us with some of the deepest realities in the world outside us and with our own will to live, to be, and to generate new life in and around us. When a character is given cautionary advice and talismen before venturing downward into these realms, wise story characters accept the aid. Brash and careless ones may be eaten by monsters, enchanted, or incarcerated by crones or devils. Then some means of reconnecting with the light and order of the world above must be found.

You have the power to descend into your darkest centers of will and courage and regeneration. As storyteller and story creator, you meet your power to give life and to take it away, to live and to die, to rule and to withdraw. The whole history of death is your inheritance, as are the vast oceans of birth and life upon the earth. As you accept your goings down as well as your risings up again, light will shine into even your darkest places. The pictures that well up from there into your thoughts and feelings will show you depths of human nature. Whatever and whoever arises can be welcomed by your wise inner storyteller.

A puppet story was made up by three girls just on the edge of puberty. I transcribed it as best I could when I realized how wonderful it was. They built the set out of classroom chairs on top of a long table and different pieces of silk which I had dyed into beautiful colors. The assignment was to make up a story about someone who needed to be liberated, and at the end of the story to have cause for a great celebration. Each group of children was given an hour to prepare their story for the others. One of the girls was resistant and anxious but her attitude and her voice changed magnificently in the course of the story. I assure the reader of this book that I did not coach this story except for the directions, though I had made the space very safe for the children's deep imaginations to work.

At the top of an overturned chair was the queen's pink upper chamber. Directly below this was a dark place filled with black and purple cloths. A silken impression of a stairwell connected them. To one side was a misty green and lavender forest. The girl who was narrating explained all this before they began.

The princess began with a grand gesture. 'This is the palace where my mother presides over everyone.'

'You may explore', says the queen, 'but you must not go to the lower chambers my dear.'

'Thank you mother.' She goes down the long, long, long spiral staircase.

'Oh, who is this moaning in such distress?' I must disobey my mother to help that poor soul. 'May I help you in any way?'

'Help me. Save me.'

'I will do what is in my power. I shall return to the upper chambers to see what I must do.'

'My daughter', the queen chides.

'But mother; it was for this kind, lonely one that I went down.'

'We shall talk about your punishment later. Now you must go to the one who gives advice to all the confused and disobedient princesses. She is true and harmless.'

So the princess went through the depths of a dark forest. The mists lifted as she moved through it. She came to the village of a wise Indian woman.

'I need your guidance', says the princess, and describes her descent into the dark chamber and the spirit she heard calling to her down there. The wise Indian woman agrees to go with her.

'You have made a wise and kind wish, princess. I am happy there are some of your kind left in this world of greedy souls. I must not let this poor spirit suffer any longer. We will attempt to free this spirit.' So

they traveled through the forest safely; the mists parted wherever they went.

'This is the palace where my mother presides over everyone', says the princess again.

'She is always performing more of her queenly duties.' They go to tell the queen what they are going to do.

The queen graciously agrees to let them make the attempt. 'Go now.' Then she hastens about her queenly duties.

'We must go and free the spirit.' The princess and the wise Indian descend the long, long, long spiral staircase to the lower chamber.

'Help me. Help me. Save me', moans the spirit profoundly.

The wise woman questions her and hears her story. 'She had been part of a good people, but others had come and dragged them down until, without a shred of evidence, she was put into the dungeon and kept there with rats running freely until she died. She is one of many who have been judged harshly, which is what can happen to most of us.'

'Help me free the poor wandering spirit with the shadows of harm upon her shoulders', requests the wise woman of the princess. They chant together.

'Go. You have my blessing. The stars are not very humble. Go and do the good of the stars.'

Then, having put several cloths on the end of a classroom pointer, the narrator said:

'This is a star of many colors of warmth and of kindness. Repay us not. Only fly forth to meet the stars. Thank you.'

The spirit went out of the dark chamber into the light and was taken into the star. 'Thank you. Thank you.' The wise woman and the princess ascended the long, long, long spiral staircase and informed the queen of the events below. The wise woman asked if the princess might be allowed to return to her village with her for a special celebration.

'Though we are small, we are very close', said the wise woman of her village. 'We shall hold a dancing celebration with all the colors on our heads and our feet and in our singing breath.'

The queen consented to let her daughter go with the wise woman, and during the celebration dance, she sat quietly in her upper chamber.

A deep contentment came over us all after this story had been told. This group of young adolescents had brought about a mysterious and powerful transmutation. Somehow, it had been a great event.

Create a sense of higher and lower in your mind's eye. Visualize or sense who lives in these polar opposite spaces. What connects below and above? Now send your protagonist into the depths and find the way to build a relationship between the lower and the upper levels of your story.

Imagine a wise guide who can safely lead your main character down into an unknown realm and interpret whatever is found there.

RISING

As you experiment with gestures and motions in story space, a vertical urge may lift you far and wide, on wings or winds or on a magical carpet. The power to rise connects you with light, joy, and vast uncharted territories, which interpenetrate your material form, reflecting into you the mighty movements of the sun, moon, and stars. The many energy centers that propel you through adventures constitute territories through which the figures in your story can ascend. The sexual realm may be expressed through powerful imagery – children born and unborn, romantic impulses, fears and jealousies, the sense of life and of death. An unhappy episode in the magnetic realm of hunger may resemble an episode in Dante's hell. As you take your adventurer into the realm of the heart, you may feel joy and warmth; all at once, the scene may seem transformed with loveliness and pervaded with a peaceful rose and golden light.

When the realm of the throat is reached, the power to speak truth suddenly may awaken. A silent one may find his or her voice and be able to say what no one else has been able to say; perhaps words of encouragement, of insight, of loving acceptance may well forth. Or, voices from even the furthest reaches of your global-self may be heard speaking in many languages. A singer may emerge as a delightful, surprising story-poet and illuminate 'ordinary' things and experiences with caring words. Advancing further up the ladder, you may climb into your thinking, integrating center, and from there into the utmost realms of spiritual vision and truth where the power to perceive and to discern may awaken into the light of ever-expanding consciousness. Story characters wandering, or compelled to go into these various realms, reflect their truths.

Through storytelling, you can safely experience the delights of going upward with wise guidance and the possible dire consequences of ascending carelessly into unfamiliar spaces. Within you coexist balance and disorder. If a way cannot be found to get down again, the heights can be as ominous as the depths. How can one master this upward urge? The proverbial princess in her tower very much needs to be saved and brought down into a wholesome embrace. The dilemma of the 'Light Princess' in the story by George MacDonald is that she cannot stop levitating. Castle turrets and towers may express a leavening sense of power, pride, and celebration, yet a wizard walled high into his protective tower must find a way down to the world of ordinary mortals. Daedalus's flight shows us the danger of flying too high too fast. The builders of the Tower of Babel strove to touch the heavens by spiraling to heights never before expressed in stone, but created instead many broken and fallen voices.

An American mother of Scandinavian ancestry wrote a powerful story during one of the workshops she attended that began:

Once there lived a bright young princess who loved to sing and dance, but most of all she loved to hear the birds of the forest sing their melodious tunes, for when she heard their singing, she would dream of faraway places. Braids that danced when she danced and dreamed sprang out of her head. She wore ribbons on her braids. She loved to wear flowing skirts so she could see the air move them like the wings of the birds above the trees. Her eyes were sparkling blue, like an ocean glistening in the sun. On her feet she wore the softest, red shoes you could imagine; they protected her feet, but the soft leather felt like velvet next to her skin.

Now it happened that she was sitting out under her favorite weeping willow tree listening to the birds when a particularly beautiful, white bird caught her eye. She was attracted to the bird and very much wanted to follow it and rose up to do so. The bird flew over meadows and across rocky fields to the edge of a dark forest. She didn't know she had come to the forest, except that all of a sudden she realized that she had lost sight of the beautiful bird, and it had grown dark. The ribbons on her braids had stopped flying. She didn't know what to do because she wanted so much to be with the bird; she started to cry.

The story adventures that followed took her little one into strange territories. Afterwards she spoke about the power of this story in her life:

I now have a way to understand the legacy I have been dealt in a very positive way. I have a way to meet it with a creative mind and not crumple or get into the syndrome of bemoaning my fate. It is truly a release to know that I have the freedom to move from a scary place. I have a way to find deeper meanings and to reconcile happenings. I can look at the symbols: when I understand them, it is such a satisfaction. The girl with the braids is going through a process; it wasn't a process that happened to me overnight. The story shows me that I have the ability to find my way. I'm not afraid to do that. I was afraid, shy. The story took me to a level that had provided encouragement, as if the spiritual side of me was given a boost of confidence. It is like the warm, comforting bed you come into on a cold night. I was spiritually comforted on a very deep level that I hadn't even known was there. The fulfilment was in the act of becoming the story. I felt as if someone was wrapping me in this wonderfully warm comforter. All along I felt totally taken care of.

Another mother, who attended the same workshop, however, had been unable to get herself out of the imaginary tree her protagonist had escaped into during her story. She had to work on his descent for many weeks. When the hero of her story finally figured out how to get out of his enchanted tree in a way that felt 'right' to her, she was overjoyed.

Tell a story in which your main character sees things with unusual clarity, as if from above, and says what he or she sees very plainly. What consequences ensue? Reread 'The Emperor's New Clothes'.

Create a set of characters who are unable to get down to earth until they receive just the right help at the right time.

CIRCLING

Children and adults who are deeply engaged with a story want to hear it again and again. Repetitions build up energy patterns and strengthen already existing ones in us. Healthy patterns connect us with the flowing regularities out of which our whole earth, the solar system, and the worlds beyond are built and maintained. In a story, a circling journey through exactly the same territory enlivens our sense of place and time. Whether large or small, covering a vast distance or concentrated in the boundaries of a little, green knoll, or a magical underground room, the one who circles through it again and again gains familiarity and strength. The sure movement of the sun, moon, and stars through the story skies, as other less orderly events unfold, inspires confidence. The steadiness of the seasons, as they care in turn for seed, root, stem, leaf, blossom, and fruit, brings a deep sense of peace and order when chaotic and terrible events must be faced by vulnerable adventurers. As in 'The Juniper Tree', wherever a true picture of the rolling regularity of things can be brought out in a story, a gentle sense of wonder and security helps sustain us through the perils that must be met.

Plants spiral upward in sure and steady circling rhythms. Invisible human growing patterns also spiral in regular increments. In old fairy tales, you will sometimes encounter a hill that can only be opened by pacing around it carefully and repeating certain words in a certain order again and again. At first the hill may seem deceptively ordinary or dull. But, when the necessary ritual has been accomplished correctly, a door appears and what has been captive can be released from those enchanted bounds.

In the wisdom of fairy-tale imagination, the winding up and unwinding of spells through exact movements and sounds may remind us of the invisible wheels through which we move and speak as we build up our human lives, releasing old ways to new. When they are correctly addressed through attention and effort, the wheeling fields of energy that are buried within us may flower freshly as beauty, goodness, and truth. As you establish in yourself the truth of the human life cycle, from this feeling of circularity, you can create circles of many dimensions. The story of your life is connected with the movement of the earth, sun, moon, and stars.

The clock of life has a round face, through which the days, weeks, months, and years continuously turn. You can immerse your story world gently into encircling realities and build your story patterns firmly out of their complex yet comforting geometry.

Tell a story about an 'old-fashioned' clock maker who loves interweaving his round clockwork and designing the faces of his clocks. Fill the story with circles and curves. Include his feeling for the sun as it moves through a whole day, and the moon and stars as they curve through the night sky. Throughout your story, enjoy a deep feeling of reverence and interest in the mighty, yet minute, movements of time.

Create a magic ritual that must be performed by turning around a certain number of times and repeating words in a special rhythm. Expand this ritual into a story that includes it.

Tell a story through which the four seasons circle three times during your protagonist's adventures.

GOING FORTH AND RETURNING

The homing instinct shapes multitudes of myths and tales, as it can shape your own stories. Neither the destination nor the return may offer perfect security, yet you can let your story line proceed with a definite linear pulse beat – a great expansion that is followed by a sure contraction and return to the starting point. The very best-loved stories in early childhood offer a warm nest of comfort. Odysseus, Theseus, Little Red Ridinghood, and the girls who visit Mother Holle go out on an adventure and return home. Father's arms welcome Hansel and Gretel home again from their forays in the dark forest. Dear Mili returns to her mother's loving heart after many years. A gate opens on to a quiet garden; familiar pets bark and whistle. A kingdom awaits its rulers; a village awaits the hero or heroine's skillful goodness. In such stories, the places and people from which the protagonists venture securely, even impatiently, await their return.

In George MacDonald's Curdie stories, when the Princess has found Curdie and his attendant beasts and other helpers, she can return health and order to her father, the King, and to all the realm. When Jason has won a powerful lover and the golden fleece in distant Colchis, he returns across the high seas to rule his own land. An adventurer such as Rip Van Winkle or Odysseus, who returns home after long years to find things very much changed, seeks to rebuild from the ground by his love. All such stories center us in our heartbeat, reminding us with every pulse that we are propelled out of creative spiritual ordering principles and powers into a life span that, at death, will return us home in good order.

As a storyteller, you can be aware that each little pulse of your heart is part of the vast trajectory of your whole life span. Your comings and goings are part of the living heartbeat of the larger universe. You can enjoy the rhythmic journeys of your story characters in this vast living context. Warm steady heartbeats awaken a sense of adventure and confidence in life. As your heart pulse expands, you go forth to unite yourself with the world around you. As you return to systolic relaxation, you experience inwardness and peace.

I was deeply touched when I first met parents who took time to be with their young children every evening. Together they had mastered a very beautiful bedtime ritual, which is often learned by parents whose children attend Waldorf schools. The whole family participated together. These fortunate children took turns entwining themselves in their father's or their mother's lap and arms. Each child was helped by both parents to remember their day. They might start with the evening meal, recall a green fly and white milk on the table at noon, then a funny morning visitor. They reversed the chronological order of the day until the children could remember waking up safely in their own house that morning. This simple ritual of remembering was followed by a prayer to inspire trust in human nature and in the goodness of the world, bringing a sense of order, warmth, and closeness at the end of the day, and strengthening a mutual sense of memory and love.

In Waldorf school kindergartens, all the children's birthdays are celebrated with a version of the following story, which can be adapted at any stage of life to the part of ourselves that remains a child.

Once upon a time there was a little angel and a big angel in heaven, and the little angel loved to look into the clouds. One day she ran to the big angel and asked:

'What is that big round hall?'

'That is the earth', said the big angel. 'Can I go down there?'

The next day she was playing in the clouds again, and this time she saw mountains and rivers and valleys, and it was so beautiful that she ran to the big angel again and asked, 'May I go down to the Earth?'

The big angel said, 'No, it is not time yet.'

While the little angel was sleeping she had a dream. (Here the teacher describes the mother and father with care.)

The little angel asked, 'Will you be my mother?'

And the woman said, 'Yes'. Then the little angel saw a man near her and asked, 'Will you he my father?'.

'Yes', said the man. Then the little angel wakes up from the dream and runs to the big angel and tells the dream.

The big angel says, 'This is the dream that all little angels have who want to go down to earth'.

The little angel asks, 'Can I go now?'.

'No, you have to wait until the moon makes nine circles around the earth.' The big angel takes her to a special place. They make nine circles. When that is over, there is a rainbow that goes from heaven to earth, and the little angel gives her wings back to the big angel, and when the little angel wakes up, she is looking right into the eyes of the woman and the man she found in her dream.

A mother, who had to travel long distances by car when her son was three and four years old, developed a story routine that was a great help to both of them. When it was time for his nap or to go to sleep in the evening, she would tell a story about a boy whose life was very similar to that of her son's. She started each episode in exactly the same way.

There was once a boy named Sandy. He was called Sandy because he had sandy-colored hair. He loved to explore and go on many adventures. He lived in a house across the street and down the lane from the shore of the sea.

In all these adventures, she said she 'let her imagination go'.

Once an old fisherman invited Sandy on to a boat and told him all about fishing from his point of view.

Another time Sandy explored a meadow and discovered that when he was quiet he could hear creatures. Even a rabbit spoke to him.

'It was really interesting what came out of the process of letting go. I always tried to tell a story based on an experience we had just gone through or were going to have. If we were going somewhere to visit, that would become a Sandy story.'

Although her son is eleven years old now, he sometimes requests 'a Sandy'. Recently when she started out with her Sandy introduction, he fell deeply asleep. After a while, he woke up and said: 'What happened?' He mumbled, she said, because at eleven, he was a little reluctant to show how much he wanted to feel the old security and warmth of their storytelling ritual.

A lively child of five was sleepwalking and crying every night after he moved to another part of town with his family. When his distraught mother came to see me, we made up a story for her to tell at bedtime. It was about their old house. In the story the old house sags and creaks when the family moves away, But, as the new family arrives with shouts of happiness and delicious cooking smells rise from the kitchen stove, the house becomes comforted and holds the new family peacefully in its 'arms'. The story worked like a charm.

Through your own original storytelling, cultivate your sense of safe return. Create a story about someone or something that travels from a beloved home and, coming full circle, finds it unchanged. 'A long time' may seem different to a child than to an adult, yet everyone experiences wonder and comfort in returning.

Create a story about someone or something that leaves a beloved home and returns by the same route after a long time to find it almost unrecognizable. You may want to imagine that your main character has lost possession of one or more of the senses, such as the power to see or to hear, yet his or her power of loving recognition may even be enhanced by the handicap.

3

Storyscapes

O gentle reader! You would find a tale in
every thing. – Wordsworth, *Simon Lee*

MOUNTAINS

Pinnacles, crags, peaks in a storyscape may remind you of your own journeying toward 'higher' goals. When we climb, our hearts beat faster, and our limbs feel sturdier and stronger. Ideals lift our heads and our hearts to new life and love and wild upsurges of energy. A lofty teacher may impart helping messages and gifts. Yet, at the top of a mountain in many old stories sits a deeply forlorn love, banished or enchanted there until his true love discovers him and frees him from his sorrow and loneliness. In European folk tradition, such a mountain of loneliness was sometimes pictured as made of glass – slick of side, impossible to ascend without magical assistance. Only on the wings of desire, by a mysterious alchemical process with perfect perseverance, could true love transcend the slagheap at the bottom and the strange glassy slopes. Perhaps an eagle carried his love upward, bearing a golden chain or cape and boots of perfected desires. This mythical mountain shines, however dimly, in all human beings; it must often be scaled through great toil and many trials.

At times mountains may also conceal and reveal to travelers realms, such as Shangri-la, that are transmuted beyond ordinary earthly heaviness. Story imagination, which travels closer to the 'heavenly bodies', may picture stones clarified like flowers, amber, emerald, aquamarine, filled with unearthly luminescences. Travelers who meet inhabitants of these realms may encounter brilliantly, intricately shining wisdom, beauty, and power. The heavenly qualities may renew, refresh, inspire, bewilder, transform those who perhaps are then charged to bring them down to familiar earth-level. Mountains may also represent mere obstacles to pass over, another solidity and awkwardness to get beyond as your story figures progress on the pathway to a further goal.

In your quest for sublime happiness, heights are discovered both as friends and as foes. They may take you up or set you back. However met, they are challenges. Guardians of rocks and streams, inhabitants of caves, and mountain creatures all inform you of their presence through your inner listening and watchfulness, as you face the heights with your story companions.

One evening a hard-working secretary and an equally hard-working social worker, who were meeting for the first time, took turns participating in each other's stories. The social worker created a character who was singing the blues in 'a deep, blue, boggy bayou'. She asked me to put my Wise Woman puppet on one hand and my Wise Old Man on the other for her story, just in case they were needed. We sensed something wonderful would happen. She draped herself and her puppet with blue cloths and got into the mood of her pre-vacation depression. She had always felt she should not take any vacations because so many needed her services. In her childhood, she had taken on the role of mother in a large and severely dysfunctional family. The secretary had overcome her skepticism and enjoyed creating her own story. Then she warmed to the role of Prince in her friend's story. She built up a beautiful, princely mountain range out of brightly colored lengths of silk. The Wise Woman and Man called for the Wise White Bird, and soon Blues Woman had been transported high into a silken valley in the Prince's mountains. There the Prince put himself entirely at the service of Blues Woman. In story language, he drew out many vivid pictures of how she could become happy and content.

At the end of the story, Blues Woman and the Prince dined and danced joyously in an imaginary alpine field of golden flowers. Afterward, both women were bemused and refreshed. They admitted to themselves and to each other that they went home and collapsed after work every day and rarely did anything nice for themselves. Out of this story adventure both the tired secretary and the tired social worker were able to make delightful resolutions to help them care for themselves much better during their leisure time.

A couple, who were having some difficulty communicating with one another, decided to experiment with storytelling. One day they chose a number of unusual puppets to play with. They created a big red and purple mountain. On one side of this imaginary mountain, the woman settled in with her lady-witch. She claimed territorial rights and grouched that she didn't want to be disturbed by anyone. A friendly male puppet came whistling around the mountain and claimed that he had bought the land next to hers and had a right to live there. She told him not to bother her. Back and forth they dialogued between his charming explanations and invitations and her stubborn defenses. After a while, he invited her to hear a storyteller who lived on the other side of the mountain. Although the witch said she never went anywhere, she very reluctantly agreed to go with him. The strange and spontaneous story that came out of this 'storyteller on the other side of the mountain' dramatically helped to put things right between them.

A boy was fascinated by mines and prospecting. When his ninth birthday was approaching, his parents, who had been exploring their own relationship to storytelling, decided to create their son's whole birthday celebration as a mountain mining adventure. They divided the birthday guests into three groups, each with a map to a place outside their house where the children could dig for treasure stones. During the festivities, they cast their son as a king and decorated a throne for him. After the prospecting had been accomplished, he would sit on his throne and accept the treasures. One evening before his birthday, while the family planned these events, the mother asked the boy what he might give his guests besides the feldspar, mica, and fool's gold that they were going to give as favors. 'Can a king see the treasure inside his people?', she asked. This inspired the boy in an unusual way. He wrote inner treasures out for his kingly subjects. The more he wrote, the more inspired he became. 'He is not the kind of child who shows his inner self', said his mother. 'But each time he spoke a treasure gift for his friends, it was like gold tumbling from his mouth'. He wrote his treasures in gold on purple paper, rolled them into a scroll, and tied them with gold ribbon. 'The love in you lasts forever.' 'You will always have good friendship with others.' 'You will have joy in your heart.' 'Humor is your guide through life.' 'You will always be rewarded when you are patient.' 'God's voice will be your guide.' 'You will be in service to mankind.'

All 14 of the richly beneficent sayings were arranged in the royal basket of the birthday boy. Each guest chose one and read it to the group. 'Of course', said his mother, 'each one was just right for the one who chose it!'. This beautifully organized party made everyone feel safe. The mother and father, as cook and storyteller, were members of the royal household. In this wholesome, imaginative atmosphere they inspired natural respect and the enduring gratitude of each child.

Create an imaginary mountain that you would truly like to visit. What is its dominant color? Who and/or what inhabits this place? How do you get there? What treasure is held there? Cast this mountain into a story. In front of the mountain, imagine two or three giants or other guards who must be outwitted or understood in order to make safe passage to the heights and depths of your mountain possible.

Go in search of a story stone. This might be made of rose quartz, tourmaline, or turquoise – whatever its substance, sense what qualities inhere in the stone. To explore different moral qualites in stones of all kinds, many books, based upon esoteric wisdom and folklore, are now available. Out of your imagination, create a story of the range of mountains from which this stone came into your hands.

POOLS, LAKES, AND INLAND SEAS

Water can stimulate mysterious overtones in your hearing and also in the hearing of your story companions, opening up a sense of streaming wonder and refreshment. The sound of water, moving gently or furiously through moss, grasses, or pebbles or tumbling from little or from great heights, deepens listening. In the tender atmosphere around watercourses, a bird may communicate to a story wanderer what he or she needs to know to move on gracefully. Perhaps fairy voices, through the din of water and wind, may be heard blending on a moonlit night. Or, in rough weather, a troll of horrible dimensions and habits may rear from under a rock or bridge to state his conditions for passage.

As hero or heroine, together or alone, move in search of themselves, a spring suddenly may feed them or from a lightly moving lake water, fish that speak may rise up. Hansel and Gretel can only return to their father after their ordeal by fire at the witch's oven by going across a mysterious cooling lake on a white duck's back. If the traveler be drawn down into the watery realm, new currents, for going inward and onward, may be discovered there, or perplexing enchantments may hold them down in the watery depths until they are freed to move on. Water-nixies, mermaids, or mermen may suddenly appear. A wild sea of crimson or stormy dark waters may have to be crossed in a storyland containing formidable monsters that help or hinder progress. A pure streaming of essential vitality may at last be discovered by a hero or heroine who has gone in search of the 'Waters of Life'.

Picture a beautiful body of water; let it speak to you. What does it need to tell you about itself? Create a story in which this body of water plays an important part.

Create an episode in which your character passes by a magical stream, well, or reflecting pool three times without noticing it. On the fourth time, however, your story quester sees and feels the reality of this place and receives an invaluable gift from its waters.

The 'Waters of Life' replenish themselves continuously. One who goes to search for them on behalf of someone in deep distress often has to endure many adversities and trials. Take a story hero or heroine on a search for these holy waters. When they have been found, bring the waters to someone whose heart, perhaps, has shriveled or whose thoughts no longer flow.

Let story characters, who are in deep distress – physical, emotional, mental, or spiritual – happen upon a very clear pool or lake in which they can see images of themselves, totally whole and healthy, reflected back. Describe this wonderful vision in detail.

Your stories may include watery bodies of different depths, dimensions. As you shape your characters to this element, they will accordingly become deep, flowing, delicate, powerful. You can feel the different moods and personalities of these watery places within the story realm reflecting your own inner fluids that continuously bathe and replenish you. Your words and images will flow more surely and fluently. 'Waters of Life' and their music well deep within you, capable of healing all wounds and sorrows.

On one of her story journeys, a rather stiff, middle-aged woman wrote of her heroine:

She could see the river coming from a golden source. She entered the water and swam toward the golden light. The river brought her to a large open space that was dazzlingly bright – golden bright. There were gracefully waving trees and grasses. Many people were coming to greet her.

DARK WOODS

Forests are found in the landscapes of many lands; you carry within you images of these external landscapes. To enter a dark forest or a thicket in a story can put you in touch with the mysteriously plant-like structures of your bones and nerves and circulatory channels. Nerves branch mightily within you, reflecting your feelings to you. Your mind is full of forests. When we experience, however dimly, the trees of Life and of Knowledge within us, we know we are on ultimate pathways of inner exploration.

The story forest is a testing place of self-recognition. As you penetrate with your eyes even a little open into the depths of your bodily sensations and needs, then you will comprehend more and more clearly the inner world of fairy-tale pictures. Going inward everyone must struggle against their primeval fear of darkness, the fear of losing the way for ever, of being consumed by strange creatures or caught in mysterious places and held there against our will.

To be 'lost in the woods' can be a fearful yet ultimately liberating adventure. You may, like Hansel and Gretel, ingeniously have to liberate yourself from the forest-witch's oven of hunger and greed. Or, you may discover a very profound Eden-like clearing within your story-self. Beauty's prince-in-disguise may live there as an enchanted forest creature or woeful monster. Great joy may be hidden in the treasures buried there or emanating from the angelic musicians who wait there to be heard by human ears. You will find ways to vanquish whatever fear you may experience as you bring your story figures into the transformative depths of the dark woods. Acknowledge the forest-like depths of your physiognomy. The warm, bright needs and energies that course through your body can be pictured and liberated from dark entanglements through your story imagination.

Picture a forest which is a dark, tangled place without a clear path, or a forest in which the path becomes obscured again and again. Smell, taste, and listen to this forest. Is it forbidding and sinister? Is it well-ordered and yet confusing? Who lives in it: a beast, an enchanter, a pure maiden? As you take your protagonist into the wood, who comes to help make the journey safe? What happens in the clearings?

Let roots, trunks, and branches grow on paper with colors of your choice. As a group of trees entwine before your eyes, notice whether your forest is empty or full, tame or wild, sweet or bitter. Is it a place of safety and protection or a place of fear and terror? Name these woods. Then tell the story of a creature or person who lives in its depths.

Aspects of your full identity can be 'lost in the woods'. Through your imagination, you can have an exhilarating adventure as you go in search of an animal whose nature can give you power, or of a primitive or enlightened holy man or woman who is communicating deeply with nature and God. Perhaps you will find a storyteller lost in your woods. Let the story of this search reveal to you your own lost powers and abilities.

BOGS, SWAMPS, AND MORASSES

Spontaneous storytelling, like dreaming, can help you to see and to resolve awkward impasses in amazing and inspiring ways. The resistance, confusion, perplexity, despair that sometimes fill every mind can be perceived freshly through a story reverie. Your youthful, exuberant traveler may succeed in penetrating through dry thickets where perhaps no one has passed before or where many have been lost or turned back. Symbolic swamps and boggery differ from woodlands: stagnation, stenches, will-o'-the-wisps, weird entwining plant and animal forms prevail – miasmic whisperings and boomings may fill the air, and there may seem to be no firm foothold.

The sense of being bogged down sometimes originates in too much food, and in recalcitrant habits or bodies of knowledge that no longer seem relevant. In storyland, as in reality, opportunities abound for overcoming the slog and contaminations in ourselves, in others, and in the landscapes we know and love. Madness, self defeat, illusion, delusion, and mental and moral asphyxiation are only parts of the whole. A symbolic journey across land that seems to pull us away from the path, sucking us down into darkness, requires stamina and grace and the powers of true imagination. A true story hero or heroine pushes on through this slime and stagnation, perhaps cheered by song, guided by a bird's pure song, or a griffon or other visionary helper. Every imagination that transforms confusion, doubt and negative emotions leads us further onward.

A middle-aged couple brought an old and trusted friend with them while they were exploring storytelling with puppets. The husband set out with their friend and two strong puppet characters to face the unknown. Almost at once they came to a boggy slough. They had their puppets grope through a tangled assortment of dark-colored cloths. The friend reached for another puppet. As she put this second puppet on her left hand, it became the 'Keeper of the Slough'. Together they all learned what the guardian of this particular bog liked and how she could be prevailed upon to transport them with her energy nearer to their goal.

Think of a habit that absorbs good energy. In addition to drugs of all kinds, obsessions and other emotional addictions can be expressed in story terms as a place of compelling stagnation. Once you start describing the habit in story pictures, the storytelling process will take you very deep into the reality itself.

Name the bog that is part of your own inner geography. Find a name for the keeper of this bog and describe its characteristics using your sense of taste, smell, and touch. You may not see it, so deep is the dark of its swamp-like conditions. Is the bog-keeper a monster or recognizably human? Have your story hero or heroine, frightened and discouraged though they may be, find a way to get around it or to enlist its help.

Describe a benevolent bird or other visionary helper who inhabits a bog and is always there to help whoever falls into its depths.

DARK TOWERS

Old stories often picture a dark, narrow, and lonely structure, that you too may wish to portray in a story of your own. This tower may be a place of banishment or enchantment for a maiden or youth who is approaching the dangerous age of marriageability. In the tower, it is as if this person must live apart without loving contact – perhaps with a witch or a scullion-boy as caretaker. The dark tower is a picture of the human body that has been walled away from human contact. Its windows are like eyes that only see a little. Living in such a tower can be a deeply sorrowful experience. Yet, in those narrow circumstances, growth forces accumulate; the one who has been incarcerated emerges with new life and form as if from a cocoon. When he or she comes forth, it is because love has found the way. Rapunzel has let down the strands of her shining hair for her witch-guardian and, when the time is right, for her true love to climb into her heart.

In the old English story 'Childe Roland', the dark tower to which Childe Roland comes is inhabited by an enchanter. The King of Elfland's tower does not see the light of day being lit entirely by magnificent jewels and captive silver and gold. In that weirdly magnetic ground, Roland's family must wait until he possesses the wisdom, discipline, and strong will to liberate them from it. In such stories, only an adventurer of great courage, obedience, and self-mastery can win freedom from the dark enchanter for his family and for himself.

Today's children struggle against new versions of the 'elf-king' whose power is great enough to shut them away from their loving elders and the wisdom of the past. Dark enchanters may hold them in weird semi-darkness and isolation until the bright clarity of our present-day Merlin-guides instruct them in the ways of self-mastery. When you experience yourself as a dark tower, you can seek within yourself one who carries strong will and determination for liberating you. Through the use of your imagination, you, too, have the power to be both captor and liberator.

A child of six, burdened with too much responsibility, was having many difficulties at school. On her birthday, her teacher made up a beautiful story to help her become happier.

A princess enters a heavy tower with a spiral staircase. She mounts to the top and looks out over the land, seeing wildflowers and children playing. When she wants to get out, however, she finds the dark tower door is locked. She feels very lonely and confused. She is found weeping at her window by a marvelous bird. The bird tells her that if she can help the guardian of Clear Spring Lake, all will go well for her. This lake had been drying up for some time. The guardian of this lake sends up wings for her to put on if she is willing to help.

For three days the princess goes down to the lake from the dark tower, dips her feet in the water, and sings and tells stories to the watersprites and creatures who live around the lake. At the end of the third day, an angelic figure rises up from the lake and sings to the princess:

I lap at your sorrows
I lap at your shore.
I lap at your feet
Till you weep no more.

From that time until this, the princess is free to sing and play at the water's edge. The waters now bubble freely, giving comfort and joy. In the waters, she finds the key to the tower.

At my fireside one evening, I asked a group of adults to create stories in which someone wants to be liberated from a dark tower. A teacher with unusual musical gifts made up a story about a princess named Aurelia:

The beautiful maiden had to be put into a tower by her father and mother for her own protection because she was so thoughtless and carefree. In the tower, Aurelia felt exceedingly lonely and sad. Again and again she tried to get out, but the door had been secured from the outside. After three days of grieving, she began to listen to the birds in the wood outside the tower window. After a time, she could also hear words in the singing of the birds; she sang back with all her heart.

One day a bird brought a gift that answered her needs to her window. The food that the bird brought in a basket was of a rich, red color.

Another day her nourishment was green, another day purple and gold. In this way, the whole rainbow spectrum was brought to her in many combinations of colors and forms. The food consoled and nourished her. Three years passed. Fed so beautifully and sensitively, the princess became stronger and stronger. Her gratitude greatly increased. Her ability to listen and to sing grew. In the tower mirror she saw new life and beauty shining from within her. One morning she tried the door of her tower, as She had many times before. Now it opened easily; she let herself out. When she stepped out from her confinement, she was met with loud cheers and a great celebration.

Two years later I met the music teacher who had told the story of Princess Aurelia in the dark tower. She remembered her story vividly:

I had protected myself by wearing black almost every day. Then I decided to connect myself with all the rainbow colors, and I could see the strength that I was gaining from them in my mirror. I wasn't frantically hiding in the tower any more. I started seeing that I was Aurelia. Intelligence, compassion, beauty – she had these with very deep assurance when she left the tower. And the whole kingdom was there to celebrate and rejoice with her. I am still in the trial, but there is an inner sureness I have now. What others think does not affect me so much. I act the way I feel, not to prove myself to anyone. When Aurelia left the tower, she was so fully there. I still like to look plain, but I am feeling more glorious. When I am in a shriveled state, I think of her. Aurelia really wears red – an 'out there' red. She stands a queenly presence. Gold is around her head and comes out of it, whether she is wearing an actual crown or not.

As for Aurelia's sense of hearing, my hearing has been opening up. She went from desperate loneliness and helplessness in the tower to communing with the birds. It was like hearing inner guidance and really receiving it. She had to take it in in order to survive. She gained almost invincible strength, dignity, and clarity. When she was out with the crowd celebrating, she could be carefree without losing control of herself. I had been stuck in adolescence for a long time, not so much in my thinking but in my feeling about myself. This was affecting the way I related to people. I especially noticed this at school because I had been feeling that it was time for me not to defer to the leadership all the time. I am one of the oldest in our music department. It was time for me to be a leader and guide. I found the storytelling challenging and worrisome – yet, it is really helpful to have created the images of Aurelia. She is a real presence in my life now.

Experience your body as a tower. Draw, paint, or make an image of your body in clay like a tower made of dark stone or other materials. Perhaps jewels or symbolic carvings are on the walls of this imaginary tower. It may be made of transparent materials and may be filled with light. Set your tower into a landscape. You might picture it in a beautiful castle garden or on a cliff by the sea. Picture your tower from the inside and from the outside, and describe it to another person in your group from these two points of view.

Create a story about someone locked in a dark tower who needs to be set free. It is probably best to focus on yourself at first in order to experience directly the benefits of an imaginative leap to freedom.

DOORS AND GATEWAYS

In many great tales, doors are pictured as more than material. They lead into new important places and levels of experience. Whether you find yourself at a castle gate in a story, at a door to a passageway under the earth, or at the entrance to the witch's house, you may feel this as an important entry into yourself. All openings and closings within you are deeply interconnected. At your heart you may feel many doors that lead to deep feelings. In your mind and in your senses, there stand doors that unlock on to vast mysteries. In your throat, doors lead to all languages, past, present, and future and to the sounds of creatures of all kinds – perhaps even to the terrific singing of the winds, the sounding of the planets, and the far stars. You may become aware of the melodic flowing of our human lives as we weave them together on the planet Earth.

In your lower centers stand doors that lead to chambers both creative and destructive. These hold the power to establish your individual self and to merge with others in order to create new selves.

A sealed chamber, which has been sealed, may open for an innocent young adventurer upon blood, violence, death. Perhaps a lost soul may wander into the locked room from which she must be saved by a consciousness higher than her own. Or, an alternative world may be entered that follows strange laws, which must be mastered, in order to return to familiar earthly territory.

Story doors may be pictured as slight and ajar; they may be heavily closed and studded with metals that are energizers or barriers. The forces of iron help us to penetrate into matter and to transform it. Copper opens to Venus' power – warm, malleable, and radiant. Silver connects us with the tide beats of the moon in the atmosphere. Gold opens on to the generous beams of the sun. A glass door may represent transparent spirit in matter. It may have a voice that is activated by human understanding and wishing. Hinges may speak, as they did to Vassilissa in the hut of Baba Yaga when she wanted to escape. Your story-hinges may be rusted, loose, or covered with symbols of the changes or revelations that are necessary for the door to open. A spell may have been recorded in the symbolic language of the door, to be broken only when someone comes to understand its messages. In 'The Queen of the Bees', a little window in an enchanted door reveals a little grey man who is holding a book in which many powerful secrets are recorded.

In your stories, you are free to seek the doors that open you up to yourself. You, too, have 'many mansions' within you. Doors may warn, encourage, or meet you with a blank stare. As you experience the excitement of thresholds, of doors opening and closing in and around you, you awake to the symbolic energies that may move through you.

A storytelling group wanted to work with door imagery. One of the participants created a remarkable series of doors.

The first door the boy encountered on his way to the top of the bell tower was of normal house size. In the upper portion of the door, slightly above the boy's head, was a beautiful carving of an eye. Just beneath the eye was a round, black iron knocker. The boy ran his hand over the smooth curved lines of the eye and admired its craftsmanship. He wondered what was behind the door.

Behind the door was too much light, and when he opened the door, he became blind. In the middle of the next door of his upward journey, just above his head, he felt a smooth softness that stood out from the rough wooden background. He felt its form and made out the shape of an ear, rounded and curved with spiraling swirls at its center. Just below the ear, the boy felt a heavy, iron knocker. He wondered what was behind the door. Behind that door was such a cacophony of voices that he became deaf.

As the story went on,

After what seemed like a long while, his right hand again glided over something rough and wooden. He stopped and let his fingers explore what felt like a door. He could feel the cold of the iron hinges and the heavy knocker. Just above his head, he ran his hand over something smooth and rounded and raised. His fingertips made out the shape of a mouth with closed lips. From habit, he wondered what was behind the door. He left that room unable to speak at all any more.

As this story progressed, the boy came at last to a final door upon which had been carved a bell. Behind that door awaited all the wise benevolence and healing that he possibly could need to be fully restored to his senses.

Resistance is a threshold. Think clearly of a way you wish and need to grow. Now experience your usual resistance to letting go and going forward to new experiences and habits. Picture resistance as a door. See the door and doorframe as vividly as possible. What are they made of? Is the door stuck? Is it locked? Then make up a story about one who is able to open the door and to step across the threshold. What lies beyond the door?

Imagine a gate in detail. You may wish to draw it. Describe the keeper of this gate, and tell a story about the gatekeeper. Does he or she have any children who help or hinder? What does the gate lead to? You may wish to imagine who built the gate and why it is there. In what way does your imaginary gate act as a help or a hindrance to whomever, or whatever, lives on the other side of it?

KEYS

You have found many keys that allowed you to move through impasses. In stories, as in life, you may carry a key for a long time before you find its right use. However beautiful it may be, jewel studded or covered with exquisite tracery or humble and tarnished, you have the key! Perhaps it has been tossed carelessly aside at some point in the story or in the story of our lives, patiently moved from pocket to pocket as we have trudged along. Perhaps it has been lost at the bottom of some mysterious lake or well, never to be found again – except with the help of another. When the key is turned in the right lock, we are then ready to pass on to a new space, level, experience, perhaps even to infinite worlds beyond this one.

The Brothers Grimm placed the short tale called 'The Golden Key' at the end of their huge compilation of stories. In it a youth must go out in deep winter snow to search for wood. As he tries to light a fire, he finds a golden key. Beneath the snow he finds an iron box that the key fits. He puts the key in the lock and begins to turn. The tale ends: 'And now we must wait until he turns it all the way and opens the lid. Then we will know what marvels were in the box.' In frozen places of our imaginations there is always treasure to be found.

Another kind of story designates a key that must not be used on pain of death or of great suffering. In 'Our Lady's Child', a child of 14 is warned not to use the key to 'the thirteenth door', but she is so tormented by her desire to know what lies behind it that she disobeys her heavenly guardian. In 'Fitcher's Bird', as in all Bluebeard stories, a wizard-groom warns his eager bride not to enter one room of his house, but burning curiosity overwhelms her. Behind the forbidden door, she discovers violence and death. Story adventurers, who discover spiritual truth beyond their depth, must suffer consequences in these stories until their wiser and more clever sisters and brothers save them, or until they are ready to admit their disobedience from which they can learn and grow.

As you seek what is locked within yourself, keys can be found. The keys in your story realm can be sacred ones. Using them with care and bravado, you may open to great and astonishing truth, beauty, and goodness.

In detail, imagine the key that fits the lock to a special chamber. For example, it may fit the lock to a wonderful room where you can always get all the rest or just the food you need. Or, it may lead to a chapel where you may go for spiritual guidance. When you know what your key opens, put it away in the pocket of a story character, whom you describe and name, for use in a later story.

It can be an empowering experience to tell the story of a noble traveler who has gone in search of a key to an important place that has been locked up perhaps for a very long time. He or she will have to overcome obstacles on the way; helpers will have to come forward to solve riddles and show the way. In the course of your story, you can discover where, and why, the key had been hidden or lost.

HUTS AND HOVELS

In the imagery of story language, bodies may be experienced as magnificent and palatial – full of many chambers that are luxuriantly furnished and surrounded by gardens of delight. At other times, we inhabit a temple of high spiritual value. Perhaps most commonly, our bodies seem relatively sturdy and practical. Pulled down by hunger and other deprivations, however, a body may turn into a tumbledown hovel. Any of your story adventurers who happen upon such a dilapidation may discover someone of great interest inside it. What is revealed in this sort of dwelling usually comes out of a mood of suffering and withdrawal. Vitality may seem debased there, yet within the walls live aspects of yourself which – though perhaps humiliated and alone – if they are truly faced may give you important insight.

You may find a saint, a good or bad wizard or witches in disguise living in your story-hovel of depression or defeat. Someone tired and old with astonishing wisdom and goodness may be in there. Or, an enchanted prince and princess in appalling disguises may be there, unable to move out until love and trust are given to them, or they are given necessary tasks to perform. Or, an angelic guide may be quietly dwelling inside, possessing the power to save and protect your characters from the worst that might befall them if they continue on their path without spiritual guidance. A tremendous sense of duty may fill anyone who knocks on the door of such a structure – a feeling that one's true destiny and tasks will be shown by the teacher dwelling within. A darkness may also dwell there – as it did for Gretel and Hansel – that needs to be overcome through ingenious, watchful waiting and service until the time is right for liberation. You can watch courageously for the dweller within whatever tumbledown, weather-worn hovels appear in your story world, and let yourself attend deeply to their messages.

A sturdy woman in her fifties set off in her story as a young woman in a cherry-colored jacket and green knickers with green wool socks.

After a while she couldn't think where she had been coming from or, far that matter, where she was going. She was in a deep, yet cheerful, forest, and it was getting darker. After a while, she saw a small cottage hidden in the trees. 'Was there anyone in there?', she wondered. If so, they might not welcome her intrusion.

Cautiously she approached the door; it was slightly ajar. She peered in. It was dark inside, and she heard nothing. She pulled open the door just enough for her to partially enter. There was a chair, a table, and a bed inside. There was one window, and there was a fireplace. A broom stood just next to the door. She drew a breath and opened the door enough for her to get inside; no one was there. Outside the wind had decreased; apparently it was not going to storm after all. Perhaps she should go out and retrace her steps to the main path. She looked around the room. There were cupboards on the wall. She shouldn't open them, but she was really curious about what might he in them, and since there was no one there...

The author of this story was clearly in an unfamiliar place and wasn't sure she wanted to continue this mode of discovery.

... Nevertheless, she went on to open the cupboards. Though the cottage was so sparse, it contained many very beautiful and rare treasures, including a thick, red book with golden writing in it. She had just

brought this wonderful book to the table and begun to read when she noticed someone standing in the doorway. Feeling chagrined and a little afraid, she said, 'I was afraid it was going to storm. I was carried away by the beauty of these things.'

The person said nothing, but came in, shut the door, and threw open her cloak. She was dressed in shimmering white with a garland of gold entwined with flowers on her red-gold hair. She smiled, and immediately Miriam felt safe, no longer afraid, and full of joy. The woman came up to her and put her hands on either side of Miriam's head. She felt currents of energy running through her body. The woman gestured for her to sit and to continue to read the book that she had selected. The words seemed to be a parable – a story about life – her life; she wasn't sure she understood the story. She probably would have to read it many times.

She looked at the woman as she drew her up and led her out of the cottage. It looked different outside. There was now a meadow of grass and wildflowers, and when she looked at it, the cottage had changed also. It was larger, more open, with many windows and open archways. She saw a building in the distance that looked like a temple and started walking toward it. The woman accompanied her. As they drew closer, she noticed other women dressed in colorful silks, satins, and velvets with pendants and bracelets like hers. They all gathered to watch as she approached. As she reached the temple, they cheered and formed a circle around her. She knew she had arrived home.

The gifted author of this story rejected it completely at first. The book of her life had been revealed to her along with a feminine image of her highest self. She thought that the story was 'old hat', 'nothing special'. Yet, the truth was that she had only written three stories since she was ten years old. The first had been several years ago under very unusual circumstances, and since no one had complimented her on it at that time, she had rejected it. The second had been in the previous month's story class. She struggled to accept that the judgmental part of her mind was not really listening to her story because it was so fully occupied with tearing her down to protect her from feeling the pain of further rejection.

Whatever 'architecture' appears in your stories, let it represent you and your language, and it will take on energy and life. Take a protagonist to a hut in a forest and tell what happens there.

Tell the story of a very beautiful palace that is turned into a hovel by a wicked enchantment. Who comes to break the enchantment and set things right?

CASTLE AND PALACE

An imaginary palace awakens a sense of life's expansive grandeur. Within its walls, in picture language you can express a vast array of roles and values. Conforming yourself to the graceful heights and architectural wings of a classical palace, or to its gardens, you feel powerful, full of matters of importance, and able to encompass family and friends as royal guests within the beauty and majesty of this domain. The lower galley can be imagined as a hard-working place, where scullery maids and cooks' boys are at the service of royal appetites. A prince or princess who enters the palace of her true love at this low level, and who works diligently there, becomes acquainted with these lower depths of human need and energy. Allerleirauh stays in the kitchen enveloped in her disguise of furs and oven soot until, in the safety of ash and fire and cooking pots, she finds courage and strength to reach up for the light-filled dancing ground of her true love. Gareth of Arthurian legends begins his quest for the Holy Grail in the bowels of the king's kitchens.

The palace depths are dark, toilsome, and lusty; the gardens are expansive with order and beauty; the upper chambers are luminous with heavenly dancing and commands from thrones of majesty and power. Whether wisdom or tyrannical whim reigns in these upper rooms is to be discovered in the course of the story. Allerleirauh had fled for her life from the imperious desires of her father to seek a kingdom more to her liking. Many sublime old stories portray these upper chambers as deeply infused with heavenly wisdom. When a young, striving soul reaches this realm, his or her garments become inwardly radiant with qualities of the sun, moon, and stars. When 'Many-furs' attains this height of courage and self-awareness, she casts off her animal skins to dance sublimely with her princely love. When you reach toward your own inmost 'Table Round' or dancing ground, there the heaviness of earthly conditions is released for a time in the royal structure of your soul-life. You can picture yourself uplifted, in the midst of the dark dungeons and dim bubbling kitchens of bodily functions, into a free space of heavenly and sublime unity.

On the occasion of her mother's seventy-fifth birthday, a painter sat down to write a fairy tale. The celebration was to begin in two hours. She had been asking herself for days whether she could give her mother a gift from her own imagination. Beginning was most difficult, but as she wrote, the story seemed to flow out of her almost effortlessly. Her story was about a noble princess who returned to the castle of her birth to overcome a witch that had usurped it. Despite the artist's usual hesitations, the elation of creating the story was so great that she read the story at the party in front of several family members. 'Do you mean I am not a queen?', objected her mother. 'No. Your mother and father were the king and queen', replied her daughter. This was a very special moment for them both. Something in the old mother's heart melted and she was able to listen to her daughter's story as a child would. She was able to love it as a child.

The artist had soon painted a picture of the castle after it had been released from its dark enchantment. The beautiful princess stood shining before it. She said of her story:

> I could finally give something to my mother that would help that part of her that I had been carrying on my own shoulders grow up. She had gotten heavier and heavier over the years. My mother hadn't been given certain nourishment in her childhood, so she hadn't been able to give it to me either. Both her parents had died when she was young. I had been puzzling about this for so long. Now I had found a way to see her as fresh and good and fully capable of overcoming the dark shadows in her childhood. The castle in the story was like her head. Now I could picture how it had been filled with darkness and how the darkness could come out and literally be turned into something beautiful.

In her story, the witch became a stone bridge in the castle garden.

The bridge arched usefully over the goldfish that were swimming gracefully in the castle waters. The noble princess could walk over it with her friends. A deed had been accomplished – a breakthrough on a very deep level had occurred. The artist had become a wise story – mother to the distressed child in her own mother, and had found heartening story images to help them both deal with their pain.

> My ideas are benevolent toward her inner child. The story has put the witch in her place. I have a much more complete sense of our relationship now. It is wonderful to be able to touch my mother in this way, and now I think she realizes how deeply I loved her as a child.

A man, who attended a puppet drama class mainly to please his lover, began one of his stories in a palace. He sat down in this imaginary palace with his main puppet, a bearded, somewhat myopic prince who was always reading a large book. The assignment was to take his protagonist through three obstacles to safety. After a time of somewhat reluctant play-acting with his scholarly protagonist, he and his puppet mysteriously began to shake. Amazing events ensued. He told us, much to his own surprise, that a palace revolt was in progress.

In his book, for a while the prince tried to find a way to quell the revolt. But soon he realized that there was no adequate advice in writing anywhere for him, and that he would have to flee for his life. He ran through the many rooms of his seat of power. Finally, he found a way out through a little back door and then he went dashing up a pathway behind his palace. His first encounter outside was with an old sage who lived on the mountain at the top of the man's chair. When he finally got this wise one to speak, he said three words: 'Follow your bliss.'

These words dismayed the prince greatly, and he went and collapsed under what he told us was a tree. For a long time he shook his head sadly, complaining about the strange advice from the mountain sage, and how impossible it was for anyone who is depressed to have any comprehension of those words. After a while though, since the story required him to push on, he told us that a piece of fruit had fallen on his head and wakened him in a strange way. Soon, however, he met a tiger who was not able to eat him up because he was now so alert. Then he was able to sidestep an avalanche. With his new powers, he eventually returned to his palace where he felt safe. He told us he could look inward now and read whatever he needed to know from within himself.

Afterwards he scoffed: 'The story didn't really make an impression on me.' His friend, a patient and kind woman, said that for years he had refused to take up any sort of meditation, though secretly she knew he wanted to. During his free time, he preferred to watch TV and concerned himself with his work schedule, and overate. After witnessing this story, she knew more about his secret, inner life. She became poignantly aware that all the components of the story were very real and authentic parts of him. In another session, this man centered his story in a little ice castle that was inhabited by 'a little, blue guy'. Afterwards when we spoke about these and other stories, he said:

It is scary and embarrassing to hear myself come out in story pictures. The puppets have the power to metaphorize my plight. I knew the blue king in the ice castle represented my situation, and I was giving myself away. I felt naked, exposed. For a moment, I was more visible to myself. The story circumvented language and my mind. I saw that no one can really be with me or reach me.

He hid in his usual defense, even though it was only a small part of his real modus vivendi.

His friend gently pleaded with him to listen to his story again. She told him that when he was expressing himself at this level, she was very drawn to him and to the energy the storytelling gave him. He kept insisting that if he occasionally remembered his story, it just wouldn't fit into his life. 'Just as long as I'm comfortable with the TV, keep my weight down, and the money is coming in, I'm not really interested.' Together they looked at his impassive defenses until, at least for a while, the ice castle melted, and they burst into an uproarious avalanche of very concious laughter.

Picture a huge structure of warmth and beauty or of forbidding coldness. Imagine someone who lives there. Take a protagonist on a visit to this palace in search of adventure.

Make a story of a kitchen maid or kitchen boy who does scut work until the time is right for rising to a greater and more graceful life in the world above.

PATHS, MAZES, AND UNCHARTED WAYS

A feeling of being lost without direction or adequate guidance is common to all human beings, especially as we cross into new territories of any kind. Whenever progress is to be made on sea or land, a way forward must be found, or perhaps cleared, through underbrush or forest. Progress requires a sense of purpose, a destination, a calling – yet, often in storyland, as in life, only a little guidance, or none at all, may seem available at first. All signposts may be covered with moss or lost to wind and weather. We may have the feeling that we must conceal our feelings or uncertainty from ourselves and from others. In stories, a wanderer may sing or speak freely of his or her sorrows, and in the midst of weeping and singing, a sense of hopelessness suddenly may be replaced with great determination. Then the right way forward may be found already underfoot – a signpost may appear or a friendly companion may beckon from a highroad. As we express bewilderment and sorrow at finding that the way sometimes is thwarted, we can listen deeply for the voices that tell our story character which way to go – or how to sit and wait patiently for guidance and strength.

I told a storytelling group an African story in which a maiden lost her way in deep jungle and came under a witch's power. She had been on the way to the village where she was to be married to a great chieftain. Captive of the witch, nevertheless she sang her true story as she sat tending crops. The chieftain overheard her singing and when he realized what had happened to her, he used his strongest magic to destroy the witch and liberate her from this dark power. Then the wedding took place with great festivities. I asked the group to make up their own versions of this story.

A young mother burst into the next class, flushed with satisfaction. At last she had succeeded in making up a story of her own. She said she had feared that she would never succeed in telling anything but a story from a book, though her son needed her to be a more inventive storyteller. Her story was about a young nightingale whose mother urged her to go to a far meadow where a Grand Nightingale was awaiting her.

On this maiden flight, she had to go across a large thicket where beautiful bird-song had been forgotten. This territory was guarded by a vicious hawk.

'O Mother, am I ready for such a journey? I have only just stretched out my wings and brought gentleness to my melodies.'

'You have only to catch the sail of the Great Wind, remembering to keep the lightness of your song in your heart, and trusting that it will carry you over the treetops.'

That evening the creatures of the small meadow gathered beneath the moon to tell their tales of time passing and to give their parting wishes to the young nightingale. She was surprised at how far she could fly and the effortlessness of her motions. Soon the color and fragrance of the meadow were replaced by the deep green darkness and heavy wooded scents of the thicket. Not much time had passed when she heard a turbulence in the air above her. But she was so enthralled with the simple grace of gliding that her thoughts quickly returned to her journey. But again the wind wavered and her flight began to falter. She took an unsettling drop; but remembering the words of her mother, she put her trust in the wind and the lightness of the song in her heart.

The light through the trees darkened as a shadow of a forbidding figure cast itself upon her, and she could feel herself sink heavier on to the forest floor. 'You thought to make your way to the meadow where I reign and join the Grand Nightingale to bring happiness there. Never! For having learned your song, I will go in your place. Your Grand Nightingale will be so blinded by the sweetness of my song that he will welcome me into his nest. And then, I will destroy him and restore the meadow to its bleakness that serves me so well.'

It was evening when the Hawk reached the edge of the woods. This was the time of day when the Hawk was in his prime. His talons laid siege to a branch, and with callous confidence, he mimicked the young nightingale's song.

The Grand Nightingale, aroused from sleep, settled on a branch to greet his love. His song was deeply stirred. 'Young nightingale, you have come at last. How my heart is filled with your singing. Tomorrow when the sun and moon are equal in the sky, will you come to join me in my nest? Sleep well, my sweet song. We will be together again as the sun rises.' Meanwhile, the Hawk, so proud of the success of his deceit, feigned sleep.

As the story went on, the Grand Nightingale heard the small song of his true love singing. Following the song, he reeled closer as though a magnet pulled him by the heart.

When he realized the Hawk's deception, the Grand Nightingale met the Hawk on his own ground three times. Though the Hawk rose on a mighty wind, it was met with the sweetest and gentlest of all the Grand Nightingale's songs. And the mightiest of the winds turned back upon the Hawk, plunging it into lifetimes of decay and mud.

As the young nightingale and the Grand Nightingale were united at the end of this story, the woman had found her own wonderful powers of imagination intact. She had conquered a bleak place in herself. 'Together', she wrote, 'they returned song to the meadow, for their generation, and for all the generations that followed. Amen.'

Present one of your important personal goals as a hidden place to which someone finds a long-lost map.

In a story, let a very tiny sign or opening lead to a place of great security, loving warmth, and understanding.

In a small storytelling group or with one other person, describe a character who is lost, and let the other(s) supply the signs that help in finding the way.

Go into a maze, like Theseus, and conquer the monster who lives at its center. Let golden thread lead you safely out of the maze.

THE HIGH SEAS

Setting out on high seas, in real life and in stories, there is a sense of salty birth. When our blood is roused, it may seem as if we are buoyed up on pulsing waves that are coursing us in new directions. Safe harbor surrounded us as we grew in our mother's womb, until a rushing current spouted us out into adventure. If you picture yourself as a boat with a mast like a human spine, anchored or becalmed, and suddenly uplifted by circumstances and surging forward, 'sails' are your strength as you find your inner direction and move ahead. 'The keel' acts as your sense of balance. 'The rudder' is an image of your will to find the right way forward, or home again, under the great holy dome of the sky.

The alarm and distress of storms at sea, or their opposite, stagnant waters, express different energy states – feelings of entropy and of apathy. A rough storm might wreck your little ship, and, in the process, liberate you from unneeded cargo or other burdens. Unloading the excess baggage in heart and mind, even for a little while, creates a sense of freedom and refreshing, spacious prospects. Then, perhaps an island of great beauty appears to the shipwrecked sailor – or another shoreline where new and important adventures are in store. A boat becalmed may be a sign that new strength is coming from some hidden source. Aimlessly drifting, neither going forward nor backward toward any clear goal, the whole boat is captivated in negative energy and doubt – suddenly upliftment may come to it. Perhaps it is rousted up on the benevolent back of a whale and bursts forward. Or, eager dolphins may sing at its gunwales, offering their guidance and help.

In stories, a sailing vessel may be transformed into a fish, like the one that swallowed Jonah in a storm and delivered him exactly where he needed to go with more speed and precision than he experienced in the boat in which he originally began his journey. Or, in a story, transportation might suddenly become a great crane or a winged dragon or dragoness, that lifts you across the waters. A griffin, both eagle and lion, might lend its fierce strength to your journey. A helping boat might appear or a saint walking out across the waters. Whatever the high seas send will be a revelation in the course of the story. Saints and angels, gods and goddesses have risen from deep within during the mythical voyages of earlier times and saved worthy voyagers. Whether the release be from a great one or a small fish splashing a new direction, there is buoyancy in such tales or episodes that are set afloat upon the great salt seas of life. As you open yourself to the connection between the fluids, which course within you and the seas and oceans of the earth, your imagination will show you the truth that flows between you and them.

One evening I asked a storytelling group to take their protagonist on a journey through water. Writing by candlelight, a very competent woman, who nevertheless had not written a story since her childhood, was overwhelmed with the powerful, mysterious sense of movement she experienced as she wrote.

She slipped into the water – really on to a large slippery object which then moved – it was alive. And she was terrified. It reared up, spilling her and the skiff into the water. It was a huge fish with red eyes that were looking at her. It turned and dove and then came up again. She got on to the skiff, and the fish swam ahead of her; the skiff moved in its wake.

In this woman's story, the powerful fish delivered her to a new and spacious, but no less mysterious shore, with a map. When she read her whole story aloud to the writing group, her eyes were shining marvelously.

A newspaper columnist was beginning a new phase of her life just as her youngest son was starting college. She was feeling lonely and anxious, yet she had dreamt she was walking with many benevolent companions along a cliff with a vast view to the sea. One morning soon after this dream, while others in a small group she had grown to trust were writing their own stories, she cast herself in story imagery. The theme that morning was one of going forward, against great opposition, to receive a gift.

Here goes! As I dive into the sea, I feel the pure waters soothe my tired shoulders and tense neck. My feet are tickled. Soon all my senses take over, and I'm wildly indulged. As I descend, the newness of the waters unsettles me. Its softness and embraces are so unlike the hard water in my parents' shower or the dismal water pressure in my house where bathing is so unsatisfying. (Largely because the boys' long, hot showers use up all the water.)

I meet a glorious mermaid who tells me I have to stay here. I can't go back to the old rough waterways; I belong here. I cry and cry and swim and cry. I am doubly cleansed. My face is streaked with the nurturing ocean waters and the waters from my tears. I dive through tides of doubt. The deeper I descend, the more alone I am. Oddly, though, I am happier. The last depth has a whirlpool. The mermaid tells me not to fear it. She says it will ease me into a new space. My gift is at the bottom of the whirlpool.

But I don't want to dive into the whirlpool. I protest. The mermaid swims right up to me. Her eyes are so close to mine that my vision is blurred. She just stares. No questions. Finally she asks me what I see in the whirlpool. I tell her all those faces formed by the ripples will transform the whirlpool into a mad eddy if I dive into it.

'Whose faces?', she asks.

'My father's, my mother's. They're both so cold. The other cold faces belong to my brothers, my ex-husband, my children. They don't want me to receive the gift.'

'Do you want it?'

'Yes, Yes. I already know what it is.'

'Of course you do. You've known for a long time what you need. You've been afraid to dive in and claim it. Now it's time.'

'How can I keep them from sucking me into their deadly whirlpool? How can I swim past them? How can I get through their torrents of rejection?'

'Easily. I'll lead. Follow me. No more holding back.' With magnificent grace she did just that.

I swam past my father. He was speechless. My mother's anger didn't have time to surface. I felt impenetrable to the others. They all had a blue cast to their cheeks. But my waters were warm and honeylike.

The mermaid called back to me, 'Open your pores!'

'They are open.'

'No, they're not! Shut your eyes very tightly and concentrate on opening your pores. You must be fully open for the final descent.'

I tried to follow her directions. I opened my pores and relaxed. Then, when I could feel the bottom of the sea with my hand, there it was. A small, handsomely etched glass bottle with tints of ink, purple and electric green. It had my name on it. The mermaid beckoned me to take it.

'What do I do with it?' 'Swim home, silly.'

'Are you coming with me?'

'No, this is my home. But I want you to visit any time or call on me in your dreams.'

I almost asked her if I'd be OK. I knew I would be now. I was still scared, sad, and confused, but now I was hopeful. Ripe with hopefulness. When I came to the whirlpool, the faces were frozen. They had become icebergs right there in the middle of the ocean. Now

I knew they couldn't hurt me. I brazenly swam graceful loops around their rigid forms. Still, I had a feeling that my new feelings were about to be tested. I hoped the bottle's contents would help.

I swam on and on until I came to the surface. I climbed out of the water and held the bottle up to the moonlight so I could read the label. It said: 'Every time you lack belief in self, rub contents all over open pores.

Don't worry about using it all at once. Contents will automatically replenish themselves.'

Take one or two or a group of children on a journey across high seas to search for their spiritual guardians and teachers.

Imagine an idyllic island and a seaworthy boat. As your story characters move toward this island, they meet up with serious opposition that must be overcome. When they arrive at their special island, they can learn in peace all that they want to know, or they can receive exactly the treasury of gifts that they are seeking.

4

Journeying Through the Elements

Apparently, there is something in these
initiatory images so necessary to the psyche
that if they are not supplied from without, by
myth and ritual, they will be announced again
and again from within. – Joseph Campbell,
The Hero with a Thousand Faces

FLAMING HOLLOW: BURNING SEA

Creative powers are stimulated whenever the great unknown is faced. A well-tried blueprint from story-lore moves protagonists methodically through the four mysterious zones of earth, air, water, and fire. Each zone presents a trial that has to be passed successfully. A hero or heroine, setting out bravely toward a great goal, may plunge suddenly into or hold back at the edge of a firey abyss. For safe deliverance from this ominous area of heat and turmoil, help is usually required. When Dante submerged himself within the geography of Hell and Purgatory, his strong and gentle guide led him through certain passageways to reveal to him the truth of what was there. Eyes more open than his could see into the meaning of the fires found in those parts. Of course, stories do not have to impart what lives in the refining realms of fire in the extraordinary detail of Dante's cosmic poem.

Our physical and our emotional bodies contain areas that may heat to fiery intensities. All manner of desires, jealousy, envy, arrogance, terror have temperatures and motions. Like Dante, we can invoke guides for our story characters as they descend into the lower depths of desire; we can visualize some of the captive inhabitants of these realms, and cast them into our stories. Our childlike inner vision senses their reality. When Perronnik had mounted the foal that knew the way to the Grail castle, he had to pass through trees in flame and a lake full of dragons. In 'The Singing, Soaring Lark', the south wind says to the youngest daughter, who is seeking her enchanted lover: 'I have seen the white dove, it has flown to the Red Sea, where it has become a lion again and is fighting with a dragon.' The Red Sea is like her own wild and beautiful blood. Astonishing help comes to the beautiful maiden in her search for her lost love. Your story figures, who pass through such trials by fire when blood is heated and destruction threatens, are likely to be greatly strengthened, like metal annealed, in the victory and grace of successful passage.

Accepting trials and troubles as challenges, your imagination will spring to your aid. It will help you perceive the burning zones that might be preventing you from meeting your true goals. With it you will discover amazing helping powers that know how to wield these fires and to deal safely with them. If you do not feel ready to harness and transform all the fiery energies that may be stored within you, you can nonetheless picture them safely in the geography and drama of your stories. Through story imagination, you can look freshly at the life powers that, unredeemed, cause suffering and death and ultimately can turn into great joy and well-being.

Picture 'the fires of hell' in a story as a burning sea or a flaming hollow. Go into the fires to liberate someone or something of great importance that is captured or hidden there.

Focus on a fiery emotion that you or someone near to you struggles with, such as jealousy or rage. Create a story figure that embodies the emotion you want to explore. As this character meets another, let sparks fly. Exaggerate everything during the struggle, for at the end of your story, both will have come to new understanding.

TRIALS BY AIR: LOVELINESS, LAUGHTER, AND THE GREAT HEREAFTER

The air is also a great testing place. When you liberate your airy self, there is often a sense of golden joy, at least for a time. In story terms, air allows us spacious liberty to explore and commune with whatever is above us – the winds, the bird-wise heights, the devas and fairies of every hue, rainbows, angels, and even the planets and farthest stars. Sudden great and liberal movements of mind and heart may be expressed through vast airy journeys, such as those that Puss-in-Boots became capable of when he had the right soles under his feet. Or, a magic carpet may unfold unexpectedly in the mind upon which story travelers may gently whir to strange new territories. An especially high flight may evoke a sense of life-after-death, when great discarnate explorations may be undertaken to strengthen and renew our inmost selves; we may visit the planets and zodiacal stars to prepare for new adventures upon the earthly or other planes of existence.

Stories that explore the element of air unground us, for better or for worse. They may heal for a time a 'too-muchness' of weight and heaviness, or they may portray ones whose lightness cannot bear the strenuous gravity of the human condition. Dangers lurk in the airy element, there being no firm footing for human beings who leave the ground, unless great support be given. In The Light Princess, George MacDonald gives us a story of a helplessly floating and giggling human child who cannot quite come down to earth. Those who linger above may learn much and need perforce to be delivered safely again to more manageable heat, watery rhythms, and the magnetic arms of earth.

You can express, through your story imagery, life beyond the pull of earthly gravity. Levity is your birthright. You can dance, laugh, fly, and sing in the brightness of joyous flight and light. You can follow the pathways of the wind and walk rainbow curves. Your story world can be filled with light and the beings that inhabit the light and the dark in vast flings of supernatural space. The night her grandmother died my five-year-old god-daughter told her mother that she dreamed that her Omi was born. She drew a picture of a baby in a purple cocoon. Above the baby was a very happy sun surrounded by delicate clouds. This was her story:

> The baby is born.
> The Baby is born.
> The baby is born.
> Omi is born today.
> The sun is shining brightly on Omi.
> The clouds are whimbering around the sun.

Take a story character on a journey far into airy space to find qualities missing in his or her life. Find a way for your character to return with these qualities and to share them.

Create a character who is unable to get 'down to earth' for one reason or another. Describe the humorous efforts others have to make to bring the airy one down.

TRIAL BY WATER

Encounters with any of the four elements inspire a sense of courage and confidence. The more threatening the waterscape you invoke in your story language, the more skilled and blessed the protagonists who pass through it must be. The resistance of the waves, winds, and undercurrents are like aspects of yourself that you cannot control until a penetrating and balanced force is found within you which, when it is awakened, knows the best way forward. Enveloping waters may threaten, yet they may also carry friendly fish, nixies, or undines who know their currents. Tides may turn, as they do in our inner lives. Furious, storming seas, whirlpools of downward spiraling energies, or stagnant and motionless seas – all give pictures of troubled waters through which protagonists must win safe passage.

A cold current may carry a coracle of hungry children relentlessly to the isle of the witch or warlock who wants a portion of their goodness. A warm current may buoy a small frail craft to safe and splendid shores. Fish may swallow reluctant travelers and carry them through under-ocean countries to a foreign human shore, where they may be desperately needed – as Jonah was – to help the people there. The peace and plenitude of inland lakes can offer, in a storyscape as in reality, welcoming quietude that quells suffering. Across the rhythmic blue sweetness of its gently lapping waters, traveling birds may easily carry weary adventurers. After Hansel and Gretel escape from the fiery hunger of the witch's domain, they are carried serenely on the back of a white duck 'across a great stretch of water' to their father's waiting arms.

I had the honor of being invited to tell a story at the wedding of a dear friend of mine. She had suffered through an earlier relationship, and I felt great concern for her happiness. I did not yet know her future husband well, though she called him her 'prince'. He had a passion for sailing, which she did not share at first. As he became the Prince in my story and my imagination informed my worried mind, I became more open and accepting of his many fine qualities. The ring, which she had difficulty deciding upon, became part of the story too. By the time I had finished writing the story for them, I was in love with both of them, and with their unborn children.

In the story, a princess grew up and swam fearlessly out into 'The Great Salt Seas of Life'. There she was swallowed on three different occasions by a wizard's fish. Inside the dark fish, she had to sit each time and guard a treasure that was inside a locked box. Many tried in vain to warn her away from those waters. I wrote:

At last a prince in disguise from a far kingdom sailed into their harbor. Full of the strength of the sea, he went forth to fish from his wide-waled boat. He was one who knew where to press upon the sea with the jeweled keel of his boat, and how to wield the boom that the sails might dance with the best breaths of the air. So as he went out, the land rejoiced, and the sky grew full of light.

After I had written this far, I felt true respect for his sailing prowess. Before, I had only felt fear for my friend's life if she were to cross the ocean with him in his small sailing vessel as he hoped she might. I was following an old story recipe for a 'trial by water'. The pattern and flow of imagery was actually giving me greater confidence in their relationship and what it might mean for her own liberation. As I followed time-honored rules, the Prince in my story risked his life for the Princess, faced the hag of the waters, and released the spell on the locked box. When I ended my story at the wedding celebration, I could speak my confidence and happiness for them through it. The story helped me to include everyone there and also the land and the sea as part of them. Everyone and everything had composed into a radiant picture.

Soon afterwards the King joyfully gave the hand of his daughter to the Prince. All the land was there to celebrate the general happiness and joy.

Above them gleamed the great golden ring. On the water, big and small fish waved their fins, bubbled, and spouted. In the air, birds sang among the branches of the trees pointing to the heights of the light. As the Prince brought forth the box of treasure, down from the golden sky spun the ring of glowing light, circling down and down, smaller and smaller, until just as the Prince took the hand of his Princess to honor it with kisses, the golden light wrapped itself gently around her finger in a shining ring. Then the reigning Prince, with his true Princess, sailed away in happiness, blissfully poised above the depths and sorrows of the deep salt sea.

Imagine a child who has the qualities that you most prize. Take this child on a real-life story adventure or a symbolic journey during which he or she must endure a very challenging trial by water.

Read the Book of Jonah in the Bible. Let your own reluctant story hero or heroine be swallowed by a great fish. Then let him or her be brought to a foreign shore to deliver important messages or to do other work.

EARTH TRIALS

Facing opposition in ourselves, and in others, we grow stronger. Trials by earth reveal grand mysteries – for where resistance is most heavy and dense the most grounded forms of love may arise. From frozen clods and out of deepest mud, lovely life appears. Together with everyone and everything, Earth holds you in her mighty grip. Your body's complex mixture of the elements connects you with mountains, fields, meadows, and rocks and stones of every sort. You are an actual storage place for all the elements.

A 'trial by earth' may be pictured as a prolonged journey through dense matter. Time passes slowly. There seems to be neither turning back nor going forward in stories where the burden of earth weighs heavily on a traveler. Woeful thoughts seem to press upon an immobilized landscape. A rider who is caught in a rocky pass may feel that he or she cannot go on and will have to die there all alone.

A trial by earth may also challenge a story protagonist with a huge field to sow or reap before a certain time or vast terrain of mountains to cross. Such pictures of ominously enchanted earth may be experienced as aspects of ourselves that we learn to disenchant. You can liberate love through the dynamics of stories – beyond the stones and ice that have immobilized your story figures is the ground from which completely realized joy may spring.

In old stories sit many enchanted castles. In these castles, what once had been living matter has lost all vibrancy. They hover profoundly apart as if they are part of a deathlike dream. A heavy sense of doom has invaded everyone there, turning living humans and creatures into dust or into stone statues. Yet, true and courageous love has the power to transform the deepest spell of inertia. After a spell has been broken, water can then rush and gush freely, fires can burst up from ashes, and fresh air and sunlight can flow into closed rooms. Simpleton, in 'The Queen of the Bees', had won the love of ducks, ants, and bees through his kindness to them. Their natural wisdom then could bring him through all the dim corridors of the castle to his true love's lips and to the seat of his earthly power. In 'Thornrose', the prince steps like Moses through the sea when the time of deliverance has come. Then the sleep of death, into which the princess had fallen together with her entire world, can wake up with great blessing and celebration.

Create a story in which a courageous hero or heroine is unable to breathe, live, and move according to human design. Think of an important way in which you yourself are immobilized – perhaps, through many generations, your family has been held under an 'enchantment'. Perhaps you simply went to sleep in yourself to escape what you could not face, or an unpleasant experience paralyzed your confidence and joy. A person turned into a machine or a stone statue may become a picture of inner paralysis. Your honest awareness of your own immobility will give your story great energy. Through your imagination, liberate the 'stuck' energy so that it can dance freely and lovingly at the end of your story.

Picture a young 'prince' or 'princess' who has to live in lonely conditions walled away under the earth. Perhaps he or she has been put into underground chambers as a punishment or for control by a powerful parent. There the young person develops a great longing for freedom, kindness, and warmth. Tell the story of his or her liberation as if it were your own story in which you are organizing your own powers and insight, and resolve to live a little more wisely and well.

Tell a story about Mother Earth who loses her power of movement in the autumn and recovers it in the spring.

5

Seasons and Moods

Every blade of grass has an Angel that
bends over it and whispers, 'Grow!
Grow!' – *The Talmud*

STORY SEASONS

The seasons flow according to mysterious and profound laws and your stories will have natural momentum as they are connected with them, carrying rich and vital imagery. Winter brings a mood of deep reflection and of yearning as the earth breathes in grass, flowers, and fruit for a time of seed-sleep and stillness. Spring sets a mood of joyous rediscovery; seeds that were lost or hidden come to light. What had been deeply asleep, or seemingly dead and gone, awakens and recovers, clothing itself in fresh forms, colors, and scents. The energies of spring can work into the coldest story heart, or the ugliest most stubborn story-form, giving a sense of tender melting, sweetness, and renewal of juice, movement, dancing, singing, and release from darkness and death.

Summer lifts spirits further, like Jack going up his beanstalk. Stories in the summer mood, in which heat and light pervade everyone and everything, tell of the longing to open and go free as the whole castle finally can in 'The Queen of the Bees'. They are filled with long, bright days, outdoor splendors, flowers, and sunlit water. Yet, they also sometimes portray the dangers of too much heat and delight. Red Ridinghood went dangerously off her path. Icarus flew too close to the sun's burning rays.

Autumn brings us down and inward again, through a smelting of iron and fire, entangling us with the vast fiery transformations in the seed-making world of plants and preparations for sleep in the animal world. When you tell stories in an autumn mood, you will naturally invoke the great mysteries of death-in-life and summon ingenuity, diligence, and fervent will to ward off attack. 'The Wolf and Seven Kids' portrays this perilous season, as do Saint George and the Dragon, 'The Ant and the Grasshopper'. and 'Iron Hans'.

The beginning of the tale 'The Juniper Tree' plunges us deep into the mysterious rhythms of the year. The child, who is to be born in the dead of winter at the beginning of the story, has the forces of spring, summer, and autumn within him. After he dies, he is held in the vast wisdom of nature and then he returns completely to life again. The circulating seasons show you pictures of your own inner life. As you blend their different moods with the progress of your story characters, your awareness of your own inner seasons will naturally flourish.

Tell the story of a tree as it responds to the changing seasons – bird song, winds, rain, temperatures. People and creatures in and around it will affect it also, as they adapt to the weather.

Tell the story of an innocent child who suffers, dies, and returns to life in the spring. Think of this child as an aspect of yourself or of another who 'died' and that has the possibility of returning to life completely well and perhaps wiser. 'The Juniper Tree' in the Grimm's Collection may be taken as a paradigm for this kind of story. An alternative story follows the life of a little seed that dies in the earth and springs to new life. From the seed's viewpoint, intimately follow the course of its transformation.

Invent a character who personifies a season in appearance and behavior. Now, have this character form a relationship with a character who personifies another season. Perhaps their interests and ways of speaking will be in conflict. How can their lives be harmonized?

DEATH

Storytelling is a safe way to let out ideas and feelings about difficult matters. In the great story tradition, death is never dull nothingess. It is an experience of transformation requiring courage, just as a wedding does. In many stories, someone who has died, perhaps through terrible suffering, takes on another form in order to help those left behind or to bring about justice. In 'The Juniper Tree', the dead child turns into a joyous bird who sings the truth to everyone in the town until he is able to resume a human form. Cinderella's mother, when she died, became a birdlike angel who appeared at the top of the tree that was planted at her grave. In 'The Seven Ravens', the brothers have to die to their human form until they can be restored to life by their sister's love and diligent sense of justice.

Another sort of death occurs at the end of stories when justice is done to a wicked impostor. Stories provide a safe ground for exploring the results of bad impulses. Children, especially, experience a great sense of relief when a very bad witch has met a cruel punishment or death at the end of a story. Such developments, however, need to be recounted with quietness, as the mysteries of true justice are serious matters for any age to consider. As in the original story of 'Cinderella', evil ones may be asked what punishment would be appropriate for whomever had committed their crimes: then that very punishment is given to them by a wise ruling potentate. The childlike part of our minds, which delights in the dire process of law after bad ones have prevailed for a time, is deeply satisfied. Conscience and guilt can consume a whole life unless they are schooled and regulated carefully. In these grand stories, the evil one profoundly knows he or she has done great wrong and needs to be punished by suffering or even by death.

In old wisdom stories, another common death experience is that of a mother soon after the birth of her dearly beloved only child. This frees the mother's pure spirit to work from a heavenly realm of watchful protection. In Cinderella's story, her mother's death strengthens their bond of perfect love. As the child faces the turmoils and humiliations of the less-than-perfect stepmother, the original mother guides her from above toward her true love and destiny, like a saint in the church to whom the unfortunate girl can go in prayer. Everyone is a child who lives between the heavenly and earthly mother, between the life beyond the threshold of death and the life that holds the child to unpleasant tasks, abuse, suffering, and misunderstanding.

In many great old stories, the reality that once was alive and radiantly connected with the beautiful young maiden or warrior is suddenly cast into shadow and sleep. All that was meaningful and alive to them goes into abeyance until the time is right for love to flourish in a new way. When Snow White is put into a glass coffin, she, like Briar Rose, is held in a temporary deathlike trance. Life goes on about her, but she cannot perceive any of it. The princess enchanted into a tower, or cocooned in a dark chamber or coffin, has its counterpart in masculine images. An eagerly questing male might be turned into a stone statue that is unable to move or speak until the spell be broken. Or, he is seated in utmost isolation and immobility at the top of a glass mountain, or stuck in a narrow cave, where only inspired love can find him and lead him back into life.

In these stories, the death experience of the heroine or hero can be overcome only when someone of the opposite gender sets out with great perseverance to break the spell into which she or he had been cast. Release from the wolf's belly, as in 'The Wolf and the Seven Little Kids', also demonstrates the surprises that life may have in store when we seem to be consumed in the dark depths of the 'wolf' or 'dragon' – deliverance comes. Some precise and helpful one understands how to undo the death: a good mother's resourceful wit, a keen hunter's penetrating strength.

To live is to experience many mysterious deaths. Each time you breathe out and draw into yourself again, go forth and return, you connect with vast rhythms out of which you and all living things are created – the pulsing of birth and death. Every story death may be deeply and clearly connected with the building up of new life as you open yourself to the mysterious laws of life and death so that they may wisely inform your story world.

A woman who had recovered from a bout with cancer created a story in which a queen had grown very tired. When another character looked into a fire with her, she said with the insight of a seeress:

'I frighten you and remind you of death, but do not be afraid. What looks like death may also be new life. I bless you.' In the fire, she also saw the shadow of the invisible demon that had been following her day and night, giving her no rest. At last she came to a stream with willow wands bathing in its waters. When she looked over her shoulder, she felt the demon was gone.

This story came at a time when she was ridding herself of the underlying causes of her illness. It was the start of a very exciting and delightful process.

The Hospice Movement encourages artistic creativity when their workers are not overburdened with other necessary caretaking. I was invited to visit a man who was dying of AIDS. His life had been a sad and empty one. Yet Hospice had created a family for him. When I arrived with a basketful of puppets, I asked him if I could turn down the TV, but he needed it on to feed his dwindling life-forces so I embarked on my story just as things were. His eyes never wandered from me and the Simpleton puppet. He lay back like a child in his bed. The story spun from its source, through me, to him. Afterwards he smiled with pure childlike happiness. I did not know if the story had reached him on any conscious level: in it, Simpleton had disenchanted the dark castle, and in the end, he was dancing and singing. I felt very privileged to have been able to dramatize a story for this dying man. I realized there is much from the realms of imagination to be shared with those who have reached the end of their lives.

Imagine a heroine or hero who alternates between living in the land of the dead and in the land of the living. In your story, tell how she or he helps in the land of the dead and why she/he is able to return to life.

Create a character who escapes death again and again by the skin of his or her teeth.

Create a shaman or wise woman to whom others may come when they long for death for themselves or for others, whether out of weariness, rage, or guilt. The wise one has the power to help them transform their death wish into new life for themselves and others. Picture the hut, cave, tepee, or other domain of the wise one. Also, picture any special clothing, wands, stones, and helpers that might be needed to help accomplish the transformation.

DARKNESS AND LIGHT

A certain color and mood will prevail in any storyscape you create – sunbeams may permeate into all the crannies, turrets, and townships of the tale. Great benevolent shining suddenly may enter into a murky chamber or a thick forest, bringing with it a sense of angelic protection and peace. Luminous, colorful jewels may fill a realm with mysterious brightness and shadows. Fog and gloom or heavy mists may press heavily on everyone and everything in a scene. Perhaps a violent inner storm or a long period of personal gloom will propel your weary traveler onward until a rainbow suddenly reflects upon brightening lake water, and darkness and storm turn into beauty. A night sky may thrive brilliantly above or glower down ominously. Darkness has its counterpart in confusion, yet night may also be experienced as a time of inward warmth and safety. Moonlight can permeate through to the breathing bones of a story world, building up a rhythmic tide that leads all to heights and depths of comforting illumination.

Alterations of light and darkness in stories are especially important to children, who need to experience steady, predictable rhythms in order to build their own bodies and breath. In stories, as in life, clear sight and balanced footsteps are only possible when light and darkness, yang and yin, work together. As you follow your story's dance through moods of shining and shadow, of wakefulness and dreaming, you will become more conscious of the interweaving of day and night in your own life. As your characters move through story moods, you can reflect more clearly and deeply on your own relationship to darkness and to light.

Colors may take on new meaning – a central character clothed in blue, pacing with dreamy serenity toward his goals, will contrast with one who flings on a bright red cape. A rogue who is dressed in green may have the characteristic quiet powers of woodland and meadow. Yellow garments may help a maiden or fair youth to leap lightfooted through their story territories. Violet may increase sensitivity of soul. Black garments envelope a seeker in the mysteries of darkness for better or for worse. Clear white clothes a protagonist in light. Clear colors in garments and jewels change as the one who is wearing them goes through changes. Someone who has passed through an important test of courage or kindness may discover themselves bathed in fresh colors and glorious light. Muddy colors, cleansed in the course of a story, are symbolic of a similar inward process.

A nine-year-old girl set her story in a palace that was equally divided between light and darkness. Her princess had been 'caught in the middle, in an earthquake, and had been hurt by both the dark and the light, which', she said, 'very seldom happens'. Imagining and presenting the princess's struggle and triumph gave this girl great satisfaction. When she had finished presenting her story to a group, I heard her say to the dark and light cloths and puppets as she was putting them back in the basket, 'You did a wonderful job. You really are invaluable.'

Though it gives a sense of accomplishment, it usually is not easy to face the dark, even within the safe boundaries of a story. In a workshop for adults, I asked the participants to write a story about the transformation of a dark place within themselves or someone else. It was at a time of unusual international turmoil. A kind and thoughtful father was appalled at the darkness his story took him into that night. His protagonist was:

> ... *a youth with purity of heart and openness of soul. The birds would sing and bow their heads; the grass would support his steps with joy in his presence. Folk would greet the lad with great cheer. Yet as he went out of the village walls, a large shadow passed before his gaze. Looking up he noticed a strange and alluring raven circling, beckoning. This bird was unknown to him, and when he asked its name, it did not answer, but flew toward an opening in the wall of trees just beyond the stone boundary of the fields. Because he loved all animals, the youth followed to learn the name of this newfound friend.*
>
> *Soon he found himself caught in a forest cavern that had no beginning. It had no end, only a circling labyrinth of direction and time unknown to a soul of purity. He cried out, 'Oh friend, why have you brought me to this place away from those I love?'. But no answer could be heard.*
>
> *'I have followed you with longing and have been brought to darkness.' A yawning cackle could soon he heard. His sight was struck by the deadened images of his friends left beyond in the field. These images began to whirl and spin and fly in his face. He heard a voice ask, 'How would you like to die? With spear or hatchet or arrow through the heart?'*
>
> *He heard himself say, 'With a hatchet', and he went into a swoon, face in the earth, heart torn from his chest. Then total darkness. Years seemed to pass...*

There the troubled man stopped writing. When his time came to read what he had written, he began by telling us about a very unpleasant incident. It had taken place in his childhood with some other boys who had started a club in his neighbourhood. He felt helpless then, and now, to transform the darkness he remembered enveloping him. He apologized about this to the group.

About a year later this same theme of violence and betrayal came back in another way. He wrote it out of a nightmare as he remembered it and entitled it, 'A View from the Castle Darkly'. In this story, a man-child, baby boy goes into a castle wall, feeling there is some treasure in there, and finds himself in a complex of passageways.

He walked to the right tunnel but turned around and walked into the lighted section of the left passageway. Then, he turned around as if being called by someone or something. A feeling of foreboding arose. As he walked toward this voice, a hole appeared in the wall, indicating another passageway leading up the castle walkway.

A grotesque, impish figure appeared in silhouette in the hole, reaching out its clawlike, webbed hand to the boy. He gladly took the hand and walked into the hole and up the passageway. As soon as they reached the top, they came out on to an open walkway. The imp with the snout of a wolf lay the boy on the ground and hit into his neck and sucked his blood dry. Although the boy made an attempt to escape, there was no hope of survival.

Again the man felt stumped by the ravening fangs of betrayal and blood lust. What could a storyteller do with these terrible realities?

Create a story that contains a vivid storm. Let this storm represent an emotion that you need to express. At the end of your story, let the light shine magnificently.

Create a hero or heroine who takes a journey that lasts for a whole day and a whole night. As this character approaches Dawn, describe the formidable characters – Noon, Evening, Midnight – that he/she meets on the way. Let your hero or heroine receive a symbolic gift from each one.

Take a character deep into the darkness where it can meet the special stars and planets of its birth. Consult an astrological manual for ideas and guidance in this great expedition.

Tell the worst nightmare you remember from your own store of dreams as a story. Ask a wise storytelling partner to transform your nightmare by continuing it as a story. Trust your partner's ability to collaborate with your story, and listen deeply to his or her words.

GRATITUDE

Virtues that you find missing in your life can be deeply experienced through storytelling. Whoever receives enough thanks for all that we give, or gives enough thanks for all that we receive? Whenever a story character expresses gratitude for a gift or kindness, golden light may fill your story. In the warm light of gratitude, an ugly one suddenly may become lovely – a stooped body may stand up straight, a prince may be able to reveal his real identity, a thing of beauty and great value may appear in an otherwise impoverished place. Perhaps a crone, dwarf, or miserable beggar receives a boon from a good soul. Although the recipient may appear unmoved at first, a power nevertheless has been released. Then, by the wise laws of story lore, the gift will reflect back to its giver in surprising ways.

Animals and elementals are often portrayed as powerful helpers in stories, especially when they have been honored and protected by human beings. In 'The Queen of the Bees', the ants, the ducks, and the bees, which were protected from harm by Simpleton, industriously express their gratitude by helping him with his other wise overwhelming tasks. At the right moment they save him as he had saved them, reminding us of the deep, mysterious exchanges in which we participate throughout our lives. As we breathe, eat, and express ourselves to one another, we are continuously beholden to the kingdoms of nature and to the greater universe.

Whenever we portray gratitude and its opposite in the same story, it will have an awakening effect. Everyone has moments of gratitude; of our ingratitude we are usually unaware. In 'Mother Holle', golden speech and life-forces come to the child who has worked with gratitude in her heart for what she has received from the mighty Mother. In the same tale, the lazy, greedy child, who felt too proud to be grateful, got repulsive speech and ugliness as her reward. Storytelling can inspire our sense of gratitude and teach us how to give thanks to plants and animals, to earth and sky. It can put us closely in touch with those who guide and guard us now, have gone before us, and whose lives will follow ours.

SLEEPING AND WAKING

For centuries, storytellers have explored the mysteries of sleeping, dreaming, and waking up. Depths of sleep and heights of wakefulness are poles through which we swing day by day, much as the sun does in the sky. We awaken to the earth's sun and to the inner sun within us, and then rest from the rigors of light. During sleep we experience mysterious regions of ourselves. In the dynamics of storyland, your tale may be experienced as a sleeping world in which everything happens as it might in a dream. During dreams the natural world is in abeyance, and we can rise out of our bodies and sometimes contact subtle, mysterious representations of who we are, have been, or may become in the future.

Joringel, in his loneliness and longing for Jorinda, dreamt that he had found a blood-red flower in the middle of which was a beautiful large pearl. He picked the flower and went with it to the castle of the witch, and then everyone and everything he touched with the flower was freed from wicked enchantment. Within the story, the dream came true – even the poison and gall of the witch could not harm him. Wise dream guidance within a story reminds us of the empowering truth that can flow to us when we wake up from our dreams. Helpers may be invited into an unsettling dreamscape to put things right. A dream interpreter may appear, as Daniel came to the King in the Old Testament, to tell the true meaning of a dream. When the right prince penetrates with love through the enchanted thicket that surrounds her, the sleeping princess can waken to know herself. In 'The Queen of the Bees', when Simpleton awakens his lovely queen, who is mysteriously asleep in the stone castle, his brothers are also freed from stone into human form again.

Because storytelling takes us into dream consciousness, it can help us to know ourselves. As your story characters rise up out of sleep, they can show you ways to integrate the strength and wisdom of your inner life with the responsibilities and routines of your waking life. You too are a sleeping princess, a stone warrior in a dark castle, until an ineffable power awakens you.

Tell or write out one of your dreams so that it is a complete story.

Create a story character who has the power to interpret dreams wisely. Where does this character live? Do any creatures attend it? Let your dream interpreter help one whose dreams are disturbing so that the truth of his dreams helps others.

Create a sleeping prince who is awakened by the courage and love of a noble princess.

YEARNING

The essential tale of every human heart is the search for enduring love, fulfillment, justice, and joy. An outcry deep in the heart may take many forms in a story. As if wrapped in silent cocoons, images of our true heart's desire may lie curled in weird configurations awaiting passage into our own story language.

In the time-honored story 'The Donkey', though he has to learn to find the notes with his huge hoofs, the ass would nevertheless find a music teacher. He yearns to make beautiful sounds so that he can express what he feels inside himself. Almost everyone opposes his search for a teacher, yet when he has mastered his lute through miraculous determination, he wins his human form, true love, and a joyous kingdom to rule. The daughter in 'The Twelve Brothers' yearns so deeply for reconciliation between her brothers, her parents, and herself that she would 'walk as far as the sky is blue to find them' and put things right. The tsar has such longing for 'the Firebird' that he sends his beloved sons to discover her ways and to bring her back alive so that her brilliance might always be near him.

Many great old tales begin with the tender yearning of a mother and father for a child to call their own. In 'Snow White', the Queen longs for 'a child as white as snow, as red as blood, and as black as the wood of the window-frame'. 'Rapunzel' begins, 'There was once a man and a woman who had longed in vain and wished for a child'. When the longing for a child is fulfilled in stories, very surprising events often ensue. So it is in real life. The man who longs for a wife may discover that when he has her, she is far more than he bargained for. Or, a proud, young woman, who is humiliated in marriage, may discover, as in the tale 'King Thrushbeard', that her true heart's yearning has been fulfilled in the beggar-fiddler who all the time had been a great King in disguise. Yearning to grow may lead to outrageous adventures. Deep yearning to sing, to laugh, to dance, to fly may unleash surprising and beautiful flights of imagination.

In stories you no longer have to deny desire. As you build up your personal storyland and as you allow your story characters to yearn after their hearts' desires, you will find new depth and perspective. You can express your very human yearning for greater health, beauty, and joy; for more power and riches; and for a realm in which all your desires may be realized. As a storyteller, you can affirm the yearning for wisdom and bliss and love everlasting in your heart's core.

Create a story about a creature who so longs to become human and possess human qualities that it overcomes all obstacles and throws off its animal nature.

Remember a yearning in your own soul or in the soul of someone you know. Create a story character with the very same yearning. Cast him or her into a story landscape. Let someone appear in your story who completely understands this yearning and helps to bring about any changes that are necessary.

Resentment is enthusiasm that has been thwarted. Through your imagination, create a story that restores enthusiasm where it was blocked or ignored.

WISHING

Your power to wish opens wide the portals to adventure. The free play of wishes spoken through story imagination allows you to explore their full dimensions and their consequences. Multitudes of tales from all parts of our earth provide a safe ground for experimenting with wise and unwise wishes. In stories, more predictably than in life, swift means of fulfilling wishes occur by magical objects or through encounters with wish-fulfilling magicians. If when I say the correct words, an object such as a lamp, a stone, a fish, or a feather is charged with the power to grant my wishes – I am suddenly powerful. Now I must learn to use this power wisely.

In 'The Wishingtable, Golden Ass, and Cudgel in the Sack', from the Grimm's collection, a youth, who wants to succeed in the great world, is given a table as reward for his apprenticeship to a joiner. If anyone takes it out and says, 'Little table spread yourself', the table immediately is covered with a clean cloth, a plate with a knife and fork beside it, and dishes with food and drink for a king. This magic table is like many magic pots, dishes, cloths, and sacks that are given for a time to story characters from which they can always take what they want to satisfy their needs. In the same story, the cudgel gives the youth strength to conquer his enemies, and the magical mule gives him endless supplies of gold. In 'The Fisherman and His Wife', a couple lives in 'a pigsty close by the sea'. At the start of the tale, the man catches a flounder that can grant any of their wishes. The ardent wife wishes for larger and larger houses until at last she speaks the wish that breaks them all – she herself wants to own God's heaven.

The sudden fulfillment of wishes can be as great or greater a burden than not to have wished at all. Through wish fulfillment in your story imagination, you can freely enjoy the unfolding of wise and unwise desires and ideas. As you speak and listen to wishes, they teach you how to use your will in league with the benevolent striving of the universe.

Speak a wish. 'I wish to feel young for ever.' 'I wish I could learn 17 languages in a day.' 'I wish I could hear the voice of the earth speaking.' Whatever your wish is, say it three times slowly and listen to yourself very carefully. Ask your partner, or someone near you, to repeat your wish so that you can hear it coming from another source. Tell a story in which someone makes a wish exactly like yours and the wish comes true.

Invent a magical word that makes wishes come true. Let this word work in your story so that any wish at all can come true whenever it is correctly spoken.

Make up a story about the results of an unwise wish.

QUESTS

Quests provide mighty blueprints for restoring ho-hum life to high adventure – every noble quest is an expedition to secure greater love, wisdom, and power. Whoever tries the quest needs to be brave and diligent in the doing of deeds that must be done. The journeys of childhood, before a sense of conscious time and purpose have awakened, are made with innocence and trust. In any story where these childlike energies prevail, there is a mood of acceptance and absorption. The little one meets sun and moon, sheep and goats, flowers and butterflies, beggar or queen with equal enthusiasm. As questing becomes more conscious and mature, goals are more defined; they act as lodestones. Does your hero or heroine seek a holy chalice, a horn of plenty, a fleece of gold, the most beautiful lover in the world? The knights of the Holy Grail sought perfection and knew that they all carried the same purpose in their hearts. Jason chose powerful sailor-mates and built a ship strong enough to carry them all to the island that held his golden bounty in a dragon-guarded tree. By right a king, he had to make the journey to claim his power.

Anyone on a mission often needs help. Some helpers may be disguised in fearful forms. A crone with croaking voice and empty eyes may at last yield the secret password to the dungeon treasure. A mangy thirteen-headed dog may be the guardian of a beautiful woman who needs his protection. Weird Rumplestiltskin saves the miller's daughter as she struggles to survive. The frightening grandmother, in 'The Devil with the Three Golden Hairs', protects the boy in his search for love.

Strange land and seascapes often arise before story figures as they persevere toward a goal. Fiery dragons represent the clement of fire that everyone must encounter from within oneself on any high mission. Heavily enchanted castles, statues, caves, ruined chapels, locked chests represent earth immobilized. Tempestuous lakes, becalmed seas, huge snoring giants rise up from our watery nature to slow down progress. Wild and surprising bird-women, witches in flight, benevolent messengers from the airy heights swoop into a tale for ill or good. When youthful adventurers are cautioned not to look back as they go forward to meet the tests that will result in greater maturity, they sometimes forget this warning voice and become trapped wherever they are unable to get free of childish ways. Their quest has to founder until the right help comes.

You yourself are a traveler who sometimes wanders aimlessly and at other times on a high mission. During the war with Iraq, I was asked to share storytelling with a group of teenage Girl Scouts; we had only three hours together. I introduced them to my puppets and asked them to create stories in small groups in which two characters would set out to bring peace to a troubled realm and one more would help them accomplish their goal. As usual, I was astonished at the goodwill and power that lived in the spontaneous imaginations of these 'ordinary' children.

In one of their stories, the Queen of India was healed by the King of Egypt. In another, a lonely king journeyed through an 'evil realm' and through great sorrow finally met his true love. Three daughters from broken homes met in a 'mystical sisterhood'. Protected by a sea star and a dove, they rowed and rowed until they came to the valley of their spiritual grandparents and were united with them. In a land of poverty where there was corn and grain but no water, a rich but good Queen of the Incas was presented with a cape of healing. She put it over herself as she slept. She felt so well in the morning that peace and health could reign again in her land.

The Princess of France and the Princess of Spain walk their separate paths toward the Stone of Peace. Hatred – pictured as a red cloth – lay between them on their path. Just when things were most dangerous, the Wise Woman was sent down from where she had been sitting upon the head of one of the girls. She guided the princesses and told them what to do. Together they dropped the Stone of Peace into the place of hatred, and peace prevailed. In each of these stories a great quest was accomplished in a short space of time.

A courageous, middle-aged woman returned from three days and nights of fasting in the desert on a 'Vision Quest' and wrote a remarkable story. When she read this story to the others in her group, they were so self-absorbed and vulnerable themselves that they failed to affirm it. Only several years later, when she had joined a storytelling group, did she feel like sharing what she had written at that time. So it is that often the deepest and most powerful expression we give to our souls goes underground, some times even for a whole lifetime, because it has not been well received by others. Her story began:

Astrid lived alone in a small dwelling in a small village. She seemed to be different from the other villagers. She stayed by herself by choice, going out only to do some cleaning or other similar work for money to buy food to eat. She wore simple, long dresses that she made herself, and usually was barefoot. She didn't know how she happened to be in this village. It seemed she had arrived as a young child – wandering in one day. A kind elderly couple, who were now dead, had sheltered her and so she continued to live in their small humble dwelling. She didn't know why she thought differently from the other young people in the village. She just knew that a voice inside of her told her to want more from her life.

One day this heroine noticed a proclamation from the reigning Queen and King of that territory: 'Whoever can find a jewel that has been lost by the King's great-grandfather will receive a great reward.' Astrid decided the quest was an opportunity for her to participate in a different kind of life. She traveled for three days to the palace. There she was interviewed by an old, wrinkled man who looked at her with kind, faded eyes.

He told her it would he very difficult for her to make the journey to find the missing jewel, but that she was free to try. Astrid told him that she wanted to try. She was supplied with a donkey and told the history of the jewel, which was 'a large, fist-sized, amber-colored diamond with threads of gold weaving through it'. Astrid's journey was a long one.

During her journey she found a little, yellow, silk-bound book with directions for finding her way to the jewel. Water, mountains, and wild weather hindered her progress. Help appeared mysteriously wherever the way seemed lost. A raven flew her over fire into the cavern that held the lost jewel. As soon as she caught the jewel up in her hands, the fire was gone, and she could return to safety with it. In the end, she was the Queen and King's only daughter who had been lost long before; that she would find the jewel when she was strong enough had been foretold.

Read the story of Jason's quest for the golden fleece. Think of yourself as fresh and untested and take yourself across a forbidden sea. Enter a fierce kingdom and win love and protection there. Receive the power to enter its sacred grove. Find the 'Tree of Life' in the grove and claim a symbol of your noble strength from its branches. Return triumphantly to sit on your throne at home.

Write out a question. Take a hero or heroine on a quest for the true answer to your question.

Think of a precious quality that you lost in your childhood. Perhaps it is a quality that was lost to your whole family. Go on a quest to recover this beautiful jewel.

WEDDED BLISS

Many wise old tales end with a great celebration of deep love. The storybook picture of joy and bliss, in a royal seat in an otherwise unidentified country, has been re-examined in light of modern psychology, social structures, and prejudices. In the process, the original gist of wisdom in these stories has often been lost. As we rise above our merely rational minds into compassionate awareness of ourselves and others, we can be grateful for the sturdy old pictures of happiness that fairy tales offer. Even after horrific adventures in so many of these stories, happiness, wisdom, and power pervade lives that resolve in a loving 'wedding'. The protagonists will have won through to a high order of life – all the varieties of wickedness put behind, they are now free to live together in harmony until the end of their days.

Jungian psychology teaches us to experience each part of a story – its characters, landscape, and inner movement – as aspects of ourselves. After whatever aeons of mysterious, rigorous lovelessness and questing, the moment of great union at the story's end can remind us of our ultimate human quest. Wedded truly to ourselves, brought into balance and harmony, we can wisely rule in our private and general castle. Such a sense of wholesome inner life, when the conflicts of identity in our modern psychological sense have been brought into creative, productive balance, allows such wise rulership to prevail. The great wedding at the end of stories can be taken as a picture of the good life realized, which radiates creative, joyous harmony to all.

Another way to see the wedded bliss at the end of fairy tales is as a picture of what is possible when two, who are truly destined to live together, meet. These two will have overcome fearful or playful disguises, enchantments, and other confusions that were tests that led them to recognize the potentialities of their life together. Whatever kept them apart, as their souls yearned for one another, has now been overcome in a great upsurge of joyous certainty. Fidelity of a very high order binds them, even in the hereafter or at least in all their human time henceforward. However we interpret the important essential ingredient of wedded bliss in the kingdom of desire, these stories help us to develop and maintain our faith in love and wise rulership as the highest purposes of our earthly lives.

Imagination tells us that we have a power within us that can transform all obstacles so that true love may thrive. In your stories you can feel free to move your feelings and thoughts toward this noble realm of love. Ever-hungry for love as you are, together with all who live on earth, as you reach toward the mystery of love through this ancient blueprint, you will find the story of your personal life also being transformed and illuminated.

A woman's imagination took her deep into a forest that was filled with soldiers who were shouting, yelling, and drinking in terrifying darkness around a fire. The king and queen had been tied and gagged in their midst. At the end of this story, a dream came to the soldiers.

Their sleep was deep and heavy. Nothing in the forest moved. No sound was heard; not even the wind ruffled the vast stillness. It was a magical night. It was a mystical night. And the dream that flowed through the deep sleep of the forest was seen by all who slept beneath its sheltering trees. Each dreamer was taken to a majestic castle high in the air. The castle was made of crystal and light, and glowed with the glow of a thousand, thousand candles. Within the castle, a beautiful wedding was being held. The king of the air was marrying the queen of the water. The royal couple stood before an altar of golden light and were united in a circle of celestial wisdom. All the people looked on with joy as the couple rode into the sky on the back of a silver snake.

In her story, the next morning everyone awoke feeling refreshed and peaceful, marveling.

The soldiers especially were struck by the shared dream. Never had they seen such beauty! Never had they felt such peace! Transformed by the vision, they moved in harmonious ranks with the good and wise king and queen, who had been freed up to lead them again, at their head.

What is the greatest opposition to wedded bliss that you know of or experience personally? Embody this opposition in a story as a witch or an enchanter. Through the power of your imagination, find a way to overcome this opposition completely.

As an example of outrageous suffering, read 'The Girl with No Hands' in the Grimm's collection. Make up a story about a man and a woman who go through similar tortures but endure, nevertheless, and in the end are reunited. As you make up your story, you may want to think of your hero and heroine as aspects of human evolution as well as reflections of yourself and of others you know.

Tell a light-hearted tale about a prince or princess who longs for love, and realizes it more joyously than he or she had ever imagined possible.

In many ways, we are all children in the realms of love. Tell an episode in your love-life as if you are an innocent, yet royal, child who is learning through experience. Somewhere in your story, suspend a powerful mirror to which your protagonists can go to 'hear' an important truth that otherwise may be too difficult to face.

6

Story Characters

This life of yours which you are living is not merely a piece of the entire existence, but in a certain sense the whole. – Erwin Schrodinger, Nobel prize physicist

GOOD MOTHERS

Storytelling reawakens childlike trust – deep within everyone lives a nurturing matrix of safety and warmth. In the story realm, we can explore and affirm the highest and best qualities of mothering that we have experienced and recreate this ideal as irreproachably wise, beautiful, and generous. Especially at the start of a story, the presence of a life-giving mother or grandmother can set a theme of reassuring stability and strength that will sustain the young protagonist through the adventures ahead.

At the story's start, she is often there in the form of a beautiful young queen who lives in a fine castle or else as a kind-hearted dame who keeps a pleasant house and garden and perhaps a few animals. Sometimes she dies in the first scene of a story and gives her guidance through birds or other spiritual messengers. In the greatest wise old stories, this great mothering soul creates a child who is good, pure, and radiant. She may or may not clearly understand the child's purpose in the story, yet she has brought a dearest child into the world through her determination and utmost love. This beloved child ultimately reigns in the heart of everyone, giving us the feeling that life is good and worth living.

Acknowledge the wise mothering presence that lives within you and in everyone. From her matrix of life-giving warmth you build your story ground, with its hills, valleys, meadows, forests, plants, and creatures. From the nurturance of her house or her castle gates you can see wise, youthful forces born and set free to wander in search of adventure and new understanding. The child of this spiritually awakened mother truly deserves the crown at the end of the story.

At the start of your story, picture a blissful union between a mother and her child. Let the child go off to seek adventure, and in the end, return to the safety of the mother or grandmother's love.

In story imagery, create the mother you would like to be to yourself and to others. Nurture this image until you see and feel qualities you would like to express more fully in your life. Make up a story about one complete day in the life of this mother together with her child.

Imagine the innocent and powerful child hidden in your mother and/ or your grandmother. Design a story in which you can communicate with this child.

OTHER MOTHERS

In reality, every good mother sometimes shifts into the role of the fairy-tale 'stepmother'. A good mother connects us with the best life-giving energies of mind, body, heart, and soul to a certainty of happiness and loving fulfillment. Other mother-beings bring about a situation of toil and hardship, of misunderstanding and discomfort, even of violence and despair. The highest wisdom and qualities do not permeate her thoughts or feelings. Inwardly she is neither beautiful nor loving. She drains energy, life, happiness, and meaning, and replaces these with sorrow and hard work without recognition or reward. Her offspring, both male and female, have cruel, hard hearts and sharp tongues; their appearances are uncouth or possess a terrible beauty. Greed, envy, jealousy, lust, laziness, and ingratitude fill their days.

The bad 'stepmother,' who appears in so many old tales, of course, resembles ourselves when we lose contact with the nurturing source of our wisdom. We can find this ravening stepmother and her children easily in fact and in fiction; especially, we can find them in ourselves. In his book *The Uses of Enchantment*, Bruno Bettelheim reminds us that, sooner or later, every human child must learn to accept our very human mothers, the ideal and the less-than-ideal mother images, that test us, abandon us to darkened vision and impulses, and push us into our larger selves to find new sources of resilience. We need vivid pictures of both aspects of mothering in order to learn to accept our own complex human nature.

You are a mother to yourself and to others. As such you discover your limitations. You can personify these limitations in the stories you create. The 'stepmother' is part of your identity. You can experience any 'stepmother' story character as a stepping away from your own wisdom and nurturing warmth. You have courage to create such a personification because you know that her impulses also belong to you, and that they can be transformed by insight, determination, and good will.

During our early years, everyone has experienced the rejection of important aspects of ourselves by our mothers and other important adults. Very few of us become adults without having our very vulnerable and sensitive artistic impulses so thoroughly squelched that we have lost touch with them. I have had to come to terms with a great deal of blank and bleak feelings that have welled up from my childhood. There was very little time or positive regard given to gentle, imaginative play in the large family in which I grew up; having no sisters, baseball and other sports dominated our family life. Both my parents were busy people. I tried to be a stoic, responsible little mother, as my mother had been during her own childhood.

At school, I remember my teacher turning away as I shyly, but excitedly, handed her a poem I had written; she evidently forgot about it. With her encouragement, I might have written many more. Of course, I never gave her another, nor did I share a poem with anyone for years after that. In my early teens, when I began to write a story, the characters and pictures that came from my imagination frightened me so badly that I threw it away. I did not know how to comfort, inspire, and empower myself through my imagination. Now I see these negative experiences of my childhood as touchstones. I feel my own pain when I meet others who have lost the way to the rich vulnerable feeling realm.

Focusing the negative and positive in a childlike story helps to clarify and open out what real feelings are. My mother did not bring flowers into the house and love them because they reminded her of her mother's funeral when she was only nine years old. One day as spring was coming, I longed to have flowers outside all my windows. Yet, throughout my life, I had felt a shadow over my relationship with flowers. I decided to write a story for myself following the precepts of this book. I called it 'The Flower Hater'.

The story seemed to write itself in a short while, although it took a few more hours for me to polish it. This story has clarified completely how I felt about flowers as a little girl. I cried deeply after I finished it and realized how sad I was for my mother and also bewildered, frustrated, and furious. I fully realized my need for flowers. I am grateful that I took the time and made the effort to express this for myself. As I shared my story with two of my closest friends, I knew in my heart that I had changed permanently, and that the process of writing it had opened my eyes. That spring I went out and found exactly what I needed for my garden without the inexplicably sorrowful feelings I had had, even when I was a child among wild flowers. I had been liberated through respecting the truth of my imagination.

The commanding power of a young person in the face of adult opposition can empower them both. In workshops for both adults and children, I usually sit quietly in the middle of the room while partners work on their stories together. Then I ask if they will share their story. Both adults and children gain energy and courage from working together intimately, and also sharing with the whole group, provided it is not too large a gathering, and a sense of safety has been very well-established. After I had met several times with a group of children and knew them quite well, I asked them to make up a story in which a child is wiser than his or her parents. Two girls made up a story about an Indian girl who wanted to help her people.

Her mother, Queen Malahara, would not allow her to go out of the castle and cross the ice to foreign shores. 'I do not make exceptions for anyone.' Said the daughter, 'I think you are more foolish than I am, mother'.

She went forth across the forbidden ice.

'This is very, very dangerous', said the guardian of that place. 'Here is the food and water that you seek. Please hurry back to your people.' When the girl returned, she called to her mother with great excitement.

'What!', said the Queen Mother, 'You are calling me! Daughter, I told you not to summon me.'

'I would like you to come with me. I am carrying water and food for all our people.'

'You have crossed the ice', shouted the Queen. But at last the Queen followed her daughter across the ice. 'O daughter, I feel so much more enlightened now. Thank you for being patient with me. Forgive me for being a foolish ruler.'

And the Queen never was foolish again. And the daughter became the Spirit of the Sun. And that's the end of our story.

Everyone in the group sat back in deep satisfaction at the end of this tale.

Think of a specific incident in your childhood when you experienced the rejection of your lovingly eager little self. See yourself in a most positive light as an enchanted but good person who has been put under a spell – perhaps held captive in a small room of a castle or off in a mountainous country where no one helpful can find you. Now, picture the one who rejected you in a creative light, perhaps as a dull ogress or as an angry witch. Exaggerate the opposition in order to be able to see it more clearly. Let the negative energy oppose the positive until the help that is needed has come and the spell is broken.

Conjure up the worst mother you know. Exaggerate her worst qualities. Perhaps you are a terrible mother to yourself. Tell the story of a mother who, for whatever reason, tries to destroy her child or children. In the course of your story, let her negativity be completely outwitted by the goodness and natural wisdom of the child or children.

GREAT AND GOOD FATHERS

Every story image can be seen as an aspect of yourself. A loving unity of masculine and feminine wisdom guards your children until they are ready to become themselves in their own realms of authority. The 'good father' is an ancient, ideal energy within you. With it you have power to command, to bless, to release, and to celebrate the achievements of younger questing energies.

Masculine nurturers and protectors are often represented in old story-lore as monarchs. The good king is the ultimate father image who rules 'all the land' wisely and well. Much is expected of his offspring, for they are the children of royal will and abundance. These fathers return from their journeys away from home with the exact gifts their offspring have requested from them. They allow their children to venture forth only when they are truly ready to attain their quests. To their sons they give the symbols of authority and power: perhaps a great sword, a sack full of gold, a noble horse.

The feudal picture of the kind old potentate may be seen even today – with the incisive scrutiny of feminists as an eternal representative of the part of ourselves that guards the realm and creates law and order – upholding purposeful patterns to inspire and guide. It is the wise ruler who knows how and when to release each of his children to the world at large, whether male or female, to seek their own powers and happiness while remaining largely in their own domains to receive suitors to their children and news of their adventures. We can experience this grand and guarding presence in ourselves, waiting, watchful, in the seat of power. Often, at the end of a story, the good ruler willingly gives half or all of his realm over to the new ruling couple with the good mother's soulful glance of understanding and approval. He may have lain in his bed of state, ailing – in direst need of the saving graces and good will of his children – until at last they have grown wise and strong enough to return him to strength, thus also proving to all the realm their own strength.

Out of a group of young teenagers came the following story, which I am transcribing exactly here from the notes that I took while I was sitting in the back of the room listening to their group presentation:

A king was mourning sincerely over his wife's death. The daughter, who shall be called Synea, did not understand. She went to him and complained: 'You are just a fake, to make yourself look good. You send me to my room so that I won't tell the others that you really didn't love her.'

While he was in his throne room, she complained about his fake sorrow all day long. One day a passing merchant in the palace saw that she needed a friend. Synea told her woe to him and invited him to return. She also told him that the rose garden would soon bloom.

Synea went to walk in the rose garden. 'How did you get out?', demands her father, the king.

'The lock was rusty', she replied.

'I will be seeing all the silk merchants in the throne room today', said her father. 'Go back to your room, but you may call me if you need me.'

The cabinet ministers and some of the merchants plotted to kill the king so that they could be prosperous and in control. They made their plans in the lower depths. 'We know she hates her father. Kill the king. Down with the king. She can help us.' And Synea joined the plot against her father to poison his food.

But just at the last moment she rushed into his room begging, 'Don't eat it, please. I know you loved my mother.' The good merchant backed her up in this and told the king about the terrible plot against his life. 'What's this nonsense. You silly mourner, silly daughter. The king your father really did care', said the good merchant.

'You nasty cabinet member, you. I am the authority in this land. I am your king. You will be banished for two years in search of a new way of life. I will send someone to find you at the end of that time. Make that ten years.'

Then the flowers were in full bloom in the rose garden, and the good silk merchant and the daughter of the king were married where the roses grew.

Storytelling can allow free and extensive exploration of themes that might be difficult to talk about in ordinary conversation, for both children and adults. Often, it is the child, who has not been able to express itself, hidden away within an adult that cramps adult life. Fears and hopes, anger and resentment of authority figures can easily be cast into fairy-tale pictures. The substantial and sensitive exercise of imagination, for its own sake, can be beneficial to everyone, like a good walk or a day at the beach.

Make up a story to defend a good father against the machinations of an angry child.

Send three sons or daughters forth to 'seek their fortune' in a story. Pay special attention to the words and gestures of the father who helps them to venture onward.

Make up a story about a good king who is ill or unhappy and confused until one of his children brings him the medicine he needs to become whole and well. Thus the child enables him to take active charge of his realm.

LESSER FATHERS

Kings, of course, may be less than wise and kind. Any father who rules and sometimes gives what is needed to a son or daughter may be deemed a king. Yet, even a king may have little to give, and must deliver his child or children to the world without blessing and love. He may, like his female counterpart, be consumed by daily chores or by negative emotions, such as envy, jealousy, hatred, sloth, greed, or lust. He may, like the father in 'Hansel and Gretel', crumple to the pressure of a less than ideal wife, and at a tender age, give his children over to the dark forest to fend for themselves. He may lose his power to love and make pacts with adversaries in order to protect his own meager interests, like the father in 'The King of the Golden Mountain' mercilessly plotting against the child for his own gain. Incestuous lust consumes the old king in the tale 'Allerleirauh'. Yet such paternal exploits are seldom depicted in traditional fairy tales, good fathers being necessary to our faith in ourselves and in life. Those who are not kings are generally experienced as hard-working figures, not present or powerful enough to prevail over the negative life of the 'bad mother'. Or, they travel through a dark wood and fall unwittingly into an enchantment because their powers of observation are not adequate enough to protect their daughters, as in 'Beauty and the Beast'. Their less than wise presence casts a hindering shadow, which, as in real life, must be overcome, on the young protagonist.

Less-than-wise story fathers make us more aware that we sometimes torment, reject, banish, or diminish the children of our hearts and of our imaginations. Yet beyond the confines of our weak, careworn, weary minds, our story children can step into redemptive adventures. So they may sometimes be able to carry back strength to the ailing kings and other father-beings who have need of their children's freshness and wisdom in order to be healed and made whole themselves.

I asked a group of adults in a storytelling workshop to go on a story quest through opposition of water, earth, fire, and air. A devoted father, whose life was consumed for several long years in researching and writing his very dry doctoral dissertation, was amazed at the story he wrote.

It portrayed a father's quest for his lost son. His main character was a wood carver,

... a quiet but intense man who worked at his craft from early morning until late at night. Years had carved deep lines in his brow; his dark beard covered a scar on his cheek. His son, however, was a cheerful, blonde, blue-eyed lad who loved to play in the folds with the animals or upon his flute under his favorite tree. He would always ask his father to come and play with him, but the father always said, 'No, I have too much work to do'.

In the next paragraph of the story,

... a cold wind, dark clouds, and a great roaring almost like the sound of a beast had carried his son away. The father heard only his final, faint cry for help. The mists and the clouds lifted, and the wind died. But there was no sign of his son anywhere. The father had to set out through the dark forest to find his son. The journey in the depths of the forest was long and hard. He lost track of night and day. In the depths of despair, he came to a clearing with a pool, at the edge of which he fell asleep while looking at his own weary reflection.

The story went on:

Sometime later, the woodcarver woke to a bright light shining in his eyes. The light grew out of the pool until it was as tall as he and took the shape of an old man with white hair and a long robe. The spirit bade him come closer. He did so, and it handed him a piece of fruit. As the carver took a bite of it, the spirit disappeared and in its place stood a swift wood-deer that beckoned the woodcarver to follow. The carver stared at the animal and all at once he felt a sense of comfort and knowing that he must follow the animal. He knelt down to take a drink from the pool but instead his own reflection saw that of his son. He knew then that he must trust in the deer and follow it wherever it led him.

In this beautiful story, all of which was written in less than an hour, *... the deer turned into a bird that flew the father across a great* *ocean. When the bird disappeared the man built a raft to go in the direction in which it had disappeared. He traveled through unknown waters for many days. A dolphin swam around a huge serpent, which was ready to devour him, and protected him. Then the dolphin took the carver on to his back. Swiftly they moved through the water to the other side of the sea. On the shore the carver thanked the dolphin who told him that his son was being held in a great castle two days' journey from where he stood. When the carver arrived at the castle, he found that his son was being held captive by the magician of an old king who, having no son of his own, had enchanted him.*

The ending of the story was a shocking one for a mild-mannered man:

The woodcarver went to the old king and demanded the boy's release. The old king refused. Then the carver drew his knife and killed him. As soon as this had happened, all the people cheered. The boy and his father were reunited and lived happily ever after. The boy was made prince, and the carver and his wife ruled wisely in the castle for all their days.

A year later when he was talking about this story, the father said that he was trying very hard to become a trained scientist but was not feeling a great connection with the work, and it was exhausting him. He had thought his quest was for scientific truth.

Through imagination people become inspired to bring about real changes. Everything is living and has soul. We can connect with our souls. This is a dimension of truth, although it is not objective in the sense of having an independent means of confirmation. This story has come back at times. I do fall into fits of depression, which tire and wear me out. I'm noticing this more. Remembering this story, I sense how strong my will is to stay connected with the wonder and happiness of my own child. I feel my power. And I also know absolutely that I would not let anyone or anything take our child away.

Create a story in which an excessively hard-working king learns sometimes to enjoy the light-hearted pursuits of his family.

Focus on an emotion or characteristic, such as greed or perfectionism. Create a story father who is consumed by this emotion. You can explore exaggeration. Set his child or children free to find other ways to lead their lives.

Imagine a wise child who is hidden away in your father or grandfather. Create the story of this child who must meet and adapt to many adversities. Tell your story with love and admiration for the joyous, playful 'inner child'. As you communicate with these childlike forces in your imagination, let this child triumph over many difficult trials, remembering that this child is also part of you.

BROTHERS

You are a brotherhood in disguise. The classical fairy-tale 'elder brother' represents your head – embryologically the first physical form to be developed. The eldest is eager to become a strong individual. Yet, invariably in the old lore, the limitations of this proud zesty adventurer become clear. He cannot get very far on the path by himself without getting into deep trouble of one sort or another. In the usual story, he rejects helpers and guides and, unable to feel his way very deeply into reality, he quickly becomes stymied in his own egoism.

The 'second brother', who ventures forth time and again from the court of the father, represents crude will. Impatient and rude, he wants his way first; his heart is closed, his head is hard. In his adventures he loses his way because of his attitude and behavior, and has to settle for less love and land or for nothing at all.

The 'youngest brother' represents all the tender love and trust of our hearts. He is kind, gentle, and often musical. At the start of a story, this 'third brother' is often found quietly and rhythmically singing to himself or playing a musical instrument by the stove. Although he is a dreamy 'dummling' or 'simpleton', he seeks adventure like his older brothers who have burst so proudly and willfully from the family bonds. When Simpleton sets out to follow their footsteps, he accepts everyone and everything he meets along the path without the fear, pride, impatience, and greed that dominate the others. Whomever he meets he befriends, sharing generously of whatever food and other offerings he may have. Often in return, he is given a gift. However odd or useless it may seem, he keeps it trustingly. Wherever he meets his brothers on the way, he gives them his loving attention, though they may mock or deride him. At the end of a classic fairy tale, this third brother is the one who wins the true princess and a realm over which to rule with her. Wisdom, love, and joy have guided his way. With his loving leadership, the other brothers can often find a better way of life for themselves.

Even in a brief, uncomplicated three brothers tale, which follows the old pattern, you can listen to your heart open up. 'Simpleton' lives within you – your heart's willingness to adventure forth openly and joyously with love. Hard-hearted thoughts and desires lead everyone astray, without the presence of this wise, fearless, and gentle one. Your 'simpleton' turns all obstacles, threats, and challenges in your story world, as in life, in positive directions.

Imagine three brothers, each with a different relationship to work and to pleasure. Take special care to show Simpleton's virtues of kindness, generosity, and happiness. In the classical way, let this 'silly' brother redeem the other two in the course of the story.

Whatever your position of birth in your own family, to move out beyond your usual sense of order through the power of your imagination is like flexing stiff muscles. Make up a long story about three princes who set out in search of adventure. The first has a very strong mind. The second has a very strong will. The third has an open and loving heart. Let the first, second, and third sons learn from one another how to find greater and finer harmony and balance in their lives.

SISTERS

The feminine triad in the old story wisdom is often pictured as two cruel, careless 'elder sisters' who must be transformed or die, and a third. You can cast your own story imagery into this universal pattern with confidence that it will work out very well. Older sisters are story entities whose antics and harshness are foils to the sweet depths of the 'heart-child'. The first two are pictured as elder so that the spontaneous and vulnerable 'youngest' may find her way around and through their oppressive angers, vanities, and jealousies. The youngest is often pictured as the oppressed servant and maid of the other sisters, offspring of a cruel mother who does not comprehend the softness and the gentle ways of the youngest and most vulnerable any more than her daughters do. This 'stepchild' among lesser women is the princess who lives within us all, perhaps, sitting in the ashes of our own self-rejections – like Cinderella, until she has gathered enough clarity and confidence to go to the dance of true love. Envy, anger, pride, sloth, ridicule, and vanity in the great old stories always lose out to her natural royalty.

This 'youngest daughter' or first daughter, by a better marriage, has often been shown to be greatly beautiful, with more than ordinary earthly beauty. Clothed sometimes in story-lore with dresses made of starlight, sunlight, and moonlight, she dances with supernatural feet. From high realms of soul, united with the deepest spiritual principles in the universe, she finds her way to earthly love and fulfillment. At the end of the classic fairy tale, the other two sisters and the dense uncomprehending mother attend the wedding of the youngest. Sometimes they have softened a little through her beauty and success in love; sometimes they remain their old selves, rejecting, even in the midst of great and general joy, the high road to sublime fulfillment. As you portray the worthy sister who patiently yearns with devotion for the true prince of love, she especially will be a picture of the willing discipline and wisdom of your own love nature. As your pure maiden moves through many trials toward the love she seeks, she is an aspect of your own soul, and of all striving souls.

Create a story about three sisters who help one another to attain a great quest. On the way, they meet a family in which the youngest daughter is oppressed in the classical way, like Cinderella – consumed by daily chores and abuse. Nevertheless, courage and aspiration are alive within her. The united sisters invite the youngest to join them on their journey. Does she accept their invitation? Why or why not? If so, what effect does this have on the family she leaves behind?

Create three feminine puppets to play with that represent the three archetypal sisters. You might also make an image of a good and of a wicked mother.

BAD WITCHES

Knowledge of evil strengthens the power of good within us. Frightful opposition and the power to overcome it are the themes of many grand old tales. Enchantresses who are evil are often pictured as clothed in dark garments, unusually ugly or cruelly beautiful, jealous, proud, desirous, murderous. They awaken wonder and terror and a certain wild joy in children and adults alike. With terrible energies, they move through time and space on enchanted brooms or by other magic, weaving outrageous spells. The palaces and lowlier houses they inhabit place weird, magnetic designs on anyone who ventures into them. Powers of speech, of thought, of love may be lost there – human freedom falls into animal indignity or mindless obedience. With a few words, witches are able to change landscapes and turn even robust humans into statues and lowly animals. The angers of wicked witches are burning hot, their appetites boundless. Not interested in kindness or moderation or justice, they can drink whole lakes and eat children in a gulp. They have grandly mesmeric, cathartic appeal for anyone whose life impulses have been overly restrained, and within the safe bounds of a story, need to be flushed out without conscience, into wrath, desire, wild motions, and dire selfishness.

In the greatest of old stories, wicked witches are invariably outwitted by the good-hearted ones who happen their way. Vassilissa the Fair, a child from the realms of civil morality, wins her freedom from Baba Yaga through giving her attention to the needs of the witch's servants. Because of her kindnesses, they liberate her from the toils of the witch. Having lost her victim, a witch may return to her own dark hovel in the dark wood to await another episode and opportunity to do her worst. Or, she may die in the same fires and torments she has devised for others.

Feminine evil can lurk in your own story realm. Yet, by the wise laws of story-lore, the good will be released from her wickedness, sometimes by their willingness to do good, sometimes by a mysterious power that comes to their aid. Any dark compulsions in your own nature – willful ignorance, greed, sloth, envy, jealousy, rage, revenge – can be profoundly transformed through your own wise story imagination.

One of ways I have gained insight into the darker side of women is through puppet-making workshops. Conscientious, kindly women very often choose to make witches, and will sew and embroider their horrible faces with tremendous diligence for hours. Our creative imagination is a great source of balancing and healing on many levels. One beautiful woman had to wear very thick glasses in order to see. She embroidered her witch's eyes with brilliant care using all the colors of the rainbow.

I was terrified as I decided to sit down and write my first story about a witch. At the time I was very angry about many things in my childhood, and I knew I would understand myself better if I flung my rage into a surge of images. The witch in my story was horrid and subtle.

When she cackled she crackled, and for years not a soul on earth knew. For the most part she lived at the far side of an empty chasm. Cold rocks closed about her chaotic binges of bitter hate and rage. One particular evening she came into a town disguised as a proud old woman with an air of innocent curiosity.

I soon discovered that she had a terrible mission and was bent on 'her favorite sort of coup'. Through clever domination, she turned a God-filled family into a numb and confusing one. As I wrote my way through the fears of my childhood, some of them came into focus in new ways. I felt protective tenderness toward my young self, especially as I turned twelve years old in the story. I wanted to be able to tell my story-child what she needed to know to protect herself from the designs of this witch, but I couldn't get through to the child. She seemed caught in the story. Yet, as I continued writing, she found her way through marriage into a hall that was filled with the beauty and strength of the greatest religions of the world. I was relieved when I found myself writing:

Music poured through the glass, and at the end of the long corridor, a single candle sent light through the whole space. Before the light was an altar made of vivid blue and transparent stone. Though in awe and overwhelmed with the intensity of this place, the young woman suddenly felt more at home there than she had ever felt anywhere in her rather short life. It was to the altar itself that she was attracted. Those who stood beyond the altar had the power to dissolve all wickedness. Each stood an emissary.

My writing stopped there. Yet the story had already accomplished its purpose for me. I had seen into myself – communing with the very real dark designs of the 'witch' had brought me to an actual revelation.

Name and describe a bad witch or two. Describe their purposes and pleasures. In a story, create a wise child or children who outwit all their sinister designs.

Tell the story of a true prince and princess who are captured in a witch's den and the work and boredom that are experienced there. Then, find a way to liberate them. When Gretel pushed the witch into the oven, she knew what she was doing.

Some of your strengths and abilities lie dormant as if under a witch's spell. Give voice to this witch within you and listen to her guile. She is a part of yourself, and ultimately she is powerless, when you awaken from her enchantment.

WIZARDS AND ENCHANTERS

Through fascination, astonishment, and even terror, whoever wields magical powers releases new energies into a story. Good enchantresses and benevolent warlocks and wizards are often able to see into past, present, and future with great freedom and depth. They can sense the arrival and the identity of their visitors before they come to their cave or turret, and they can give wise, if cryptic, advice and warning. Sometimes they speak in verse or with old language and gestures. Although usually pictured as aged with experience, like Merlin, and strong of feature, they are sometimes seen as youthful. The Founder of the Universe in George MacDonald's *The Golden Key* is pictured as a newborn babe.

Magicians' clothing may be rough or strange to set them apart, their homes may be situated in solitary byways, along mountain paths or in deep forest glades. In storyland, as in life, these clairvoyant enchanter-gurus await those who are seeking new depths and heights of understanding about themselves and the universe. Seekers abide a while with them, losing their usual sense of time and space until, having learned the lessons they needed and having received necessary gifts, they pass on to greater adventures.

Benevolent wizard-teachers give exactly the new impetus an adventurer requires. Nasty enchanters, like their feminine counterparts, cast strenuous spells over young adventurers and over whole kingdoms, forests, and glens. They are often found conniving to extend their constraining powers into otherwise happy realms. Their unsuspecting guests may suddenly be changed into repugnant shapes or have heavy conditions set on their lives. If the enchanters are longing to be released from the toil of evil in their own souls by true love, their spells may burden families and whole kingdoms for years until the strength can be found to illuminate their ugliness and destructive might with the truth of love.

Your story world is a theater for your soul-life. You can very courageously and deliberately create a place in your imagination where your characters may go in order to be healed and helped by a benevolent sage. You can also deliberately allow room for negative enchanters to work so that you and your audience may recognize the many disguises of evil in the real world. People and places put under spells, human beings turned into animals or stones, souls reduced to ineffectuality or darkly caught in bondage, show you aspects of yourself and of others that can be positively transformed.

The following puppet story was created by two imaginative girls of ten in an after-school program at a public school not far from my home. One of the girls, who acted as its narrator, is of Irish descent and has the special gift of connecting inner vision and poetic speech. They called their story 'The Cave of Pools'.

'These Pools are the World', crooned the narrator with a grand gesture over their stage – blue and hazy grey cloths draped over a school table with overturned chairs on it. 'These are the Caves of Misery and the Caves of Glad Happiness. All caves are variations of these. I am the Gnome that takes care of these caves. If you enter this Cave of Misery, you will feel dulled or nothing at all except a dome of sticky haze. O a knock. What's that?'

An evil wizard entered the scene. 'I told you this was a tricky job', said the Gnome, hiding to protect himself from his evil ways.

The wizard took possession of the Caves. 'Ha!', said the wizard, 'I'll take all these pools of Misery and Happiness and muddle them together.

Then I can collect the haze. I have all the magic I need. Ha! Now, I am Ruler of the Land. None shall laugh.'

A kind young prince wants to free the Caves from evil. He secretly enters into them. 'I must keep a clear mind and heart lest evil engulf me. There is only one way to save the world. The only hope is the buried Necklace of Happiness. I know it is somewhere here on top of this dried sea. Oh, muddleglum, I must not bite a bit or sip a sup lest evil engulf me.'

The narrator brought out another puppet, saying: 'This boy came out of the dark forest and was blinded by light. He fell into the Pools and was engulfed by them.'

The boy and the kind prince met in whispers: 'O this is such a confusing place. I am a young boy. I was raised by animals. I hope I can trust you, Prince. You have not the ignorance of these others who are captivated in the haze.'

'Together they searched and searched for the Necklace of the Living, Happy World', continued the narrator:

'The Necklace is our only hope', said the prince. 'O I am so hungry, so thirsty. Days and nights have passed. Ah, the Cave. Sshh – or the wizard may see me. It looks safe enough now. Ah, I have found a rainbow necklace. It is the Necklace of the Living World! Look, the gloom is gone! Now let all evil he banished.'

'Ah, I have all the magic', shouts the evil wizard. 'All, except ours!'
'The evilness was lifted', said the narrator. 'The wizard was lifted with

it, but he fell back because evil is heavy.' Then to the Cave of Pools on top of the dry sea – so heavy, so hot – returned the Light', said the narrator in a low and powerful voice. Her partner in the drama unfurled a bright cloth over the hazy ones.

'Now you must take good care of these magical Pools always', said the Gnome to the boy and the prince. 'I will show you how.'

These children had brought about a metaphysical drama that moved me to tears. I continue to wonder at the tremendous courage and caring wisdom that wells from children when they are given a safe and creative space to express themselves. Of course, the puppets and the beautifully colored silk cloths helped them to feel in touch with their deepest selves while playacting. An adult can easily be distracted from these wise depths by many varieties of cleverness and hazy confusion. Yet, when given at least half a chance, the wise child within you can play out great drama like these children did.

I was honored to make up a birthday story about a wizard for a very energetic seven-year-old eldest child who loved the woods. Her mother asked that her story be very imaginative because she feared that her daughter was becoming too literal and matter-of-fact. The heroine was named 'Princess Starfire' and she was the youngest child of a good King and Queen who had many children.

Princess Starfire Mathilde begged to attend every possible festivity and celebration and to make them brighter with the flowers she brought and the candles she decorated. Many moons passed over the palace rooftops as she grew older and bolder.

One day when she almost had reached the ripe age of seven years old, a messenger spoke sadly. 'If something is not done at once, the Royal Wood will be no more, and the wold-wizard will die.'

'Oh woe', wept the Queen, wringing her hands.

'I must call a council', announced the King, stroking his long white beard. When the King's best counsellors had arrived, the King said: 'Now my youngest princess, under no circumstances are you to leave your own room. The times are grave, and we are not to be disturbed.' With that he closed the heavy door of state.

Princess Starfire, who was a true princess and obedient in her heart, scowled and strode slowly to her room. There she sat for a long time, glumly, with her chin on her fist. She threw a red slipper against her door, then another. Suddenly, a little brown mouse who was wearing a tiny green hat scurried up to her feet.

'Follow me!', it squeaked with musical timbre. 'Follow me to the wizard's wold.' Princess Starfire could not believe her eyes or her ears. 'Follow me', it repeated.

'But I am not allowed to go into the forest alone.'

'I will protect ye. Come with me to the wizard's tree. It is his wish and his decree', squeaked the mouse.

As the story progressed, the princess met the old wizard of the wood whose life had been confined to a hollow tree from which he could not find enough strength to move.

'What am I to do?', she offered, with great willingness.

'Sit down and I will tell you.' Though Princess Starfire did not want to sit, she obeyed him nevertheless. 'When I was young, the birds sang here in abundance; all the fairies of north, south, east, and west came at my command with their helping wings and invisible singing. Trees of all varieties could thrive. Now the woods are dying, and I no longer can do my work alone.' He paused and looked at her deeply for a long time until she felt quite uncomfortable. 'I have heard from the mouse that you have a great way with singing and with celebration.'

'O yes', she nodded.

'Good', said he. 'I believed you would be willing to help us.' She nodded again, with determination. 'Under this tree is my calling stone.'

As the story went on, the princess summoned helpers with her strong human voice. As she sang they circled, jubilating around them.

'Whenever you hold a calling-stone and sing with love in your heart, though you may not see me, I will be near', said the wold-wizard, 'and my wood fairies and my gnomes will be close to me.' He told her many

ways she and her human sisters and brothers might help to clear the woodlands and encourage trees to spring up again.

Then the wizard was gone... and the little brown mouse with the green hat said, as if he had learned his rhyme from the wold-wizard himself: 'Human princess, so patient and so true. Quickly follow! Keep me in view!' And so he led her back through thorny places and thickets and past old strewn logs and twigs, across the great open meadow and once again into her own palace room.

From that day on, Princess Starfire brought many children into her forest. She showed them how to stand still and watch for the delicate dancing of the fairies in all seasons, and to sing to the gnomes at work in their underground. From that time on, the woods filled with every sort of woodlife...

When Princess Starfire was grown up and had brought her own babies to birth, with bright stars in their eyes, she still went out to the wizard's wold to listen, to watch, and to teach them to sing for the wizard who, it was said, now would never need to die. And every year as queen she held a great festival in honor of the wizard-of-the-wold and all his kind.

Picture the greatest opposition in your life as a wicked wizard. Describe this wizard with a few telling details. Now create the character who can circumscribe the wizard's spell. Pit these two against one another in a story that lasts no more than seven minutes. Be sure to work with a partner who will help you to listen to your story as you tell it. Keep going until the spell is broken.

Tell a story about a benevolent wizard who has lost his powers because human beings no longer respect them. A good source of inspiration is Michael Ende's *The Never-Ending Story*.

TRICKSTERS AND JESTERS

Traditional 'tricksters' are able to outwit anyone they choose to dominate. Combative, competitive, like a young dog or lion, they inspire a sense of wild, even cosmic, bravado. The game – to get the better of the other, whether friend or foe, by whatever means is not necessarily edifying. Sometimes they get into wild adventures and fail; yet they remain inordinately proud of their exploits and if necessary, loudly boast and crow to disguise their failures. In stories when fragile human beings are threatened or suffering, they turn to these phenomenal tricksters for help. Raven of the Northwest Pacific Indians is like a god, at times capable of anything, yet he is imperfect and so the innocent cause of earthly imperfections. He always enters boldly into a dilemma or fray. Overconfident, greedy, and thoughtless, things often become very difficult for him, although in the end his determination and unusual powers prevail.

Jesters tumble in and out of the shadows of story – potentates who must, because of their duties, remain full of dignity and 'wise' restraint. Through their wild, playful language, mockery, songs, dances, and whimsy, they bring antic energies into a story and open out playful perspectives on all the story's characters and events. A jester might change hats with a king or princess for a time in order to give him or her an opportunity to sing or to dance, for once, on the wild green.

You can seek within your story-self the trickster who has the will to combat any opposition and to feel creativity and pride without limit. His crude energy will challenge your own restraining games. You can also welcome a playful jester into your story world who can jauntily debunk any excessive propriety in the characters that you invent.

Picture the greatest opposition to your own health and well-being. Dress it up as a story character and give it a terrible and outrageous name. Now, describe it with a few details. For example: How big are its feet and mouth? How does it move? What is its favorite gesture? What kind of sounds does it make? Freely exaggerate anything and everything. Then create a 'trickster' who can outwit it perfectly. Describe this trickster in loving detail. How does it get its way?

In the court of a serious and high-minded king, queen, or royal child, invent a jester or clown who makes great fun of their excessively proud and responsible rituals. When the ruling potentates want to go to war, with what antics does your jester entertain them?

COOKS

You are a child of earth who must be nourished in order to live. The giving and receiving of food and drink in stories can show you food of death and food of life – denial, greed, and wise discipline; meals of dust and famine; feasts of starlight and purest love. Story cooks, young and old, male and female, busy themselves with substances from all realms of nature. Because of their task, a fish or fowl may leap up and speak to them. They are often pictured as good-humored and very well-fed themselves. A worthy one gives exactly what is needed to the weary passerby.

The wise woman in George MacDonald's *The Golden Key* is typical of those who, in offering bread and wine or milk, give a sacrament of healing. A cook may possess the wisdom of an angel and in a glance gives forth perfect nourishment. A less than good cook might offer food that harms the innocent, striving soul at the center of the story. Being rather stupid or else from some conscious intent to harm, such a cook or purveyor of food may have an evil gleam, like the jealous queen did when she offered the poisoned apple to Snow White and like the witch in the story of 'Hansel and Gretel'.

The fire of a home stove can be a place of dreamy comfort and nurturance. The 'third child' of classic fairy tales, whose heart is strong and pure, is often pictured in close connection with this substitute mother, who is a steady, secure source of warmth. Unlike modern electric stoves the old ones were always kept stoked. But stove fires may also become a dire threat, as in the home of a giant or witch, where children may be cooked and eaten.

At first in stories, as in life, a child is entirely at the mercy of others for nourishment. Gradually this helplessness is overcome. Sometimes a child becomes a cook's assistant in a story – learning to select, to prepare, and to serve food awakens awareness and discrimination in many other areas of life. Allerleirauh learns to make a sublime soup so that her true love may recognize her. Gareth, when he serves King Arthur and his court as cook's boy, is preparing for other tasks and challenges.

Often a story character must learn to deny food for a time, practicing an austerity that brings about a specific liberation. In the old English story 'Childe Roland', the youngest son remembers Merlin's warning to take no food in Elfland; so he wins the battle with the elf-king and brings his beloved sister and brothers back to life. To eat is often to become enchanted, even to die, unless only the right food be taken under the right circumstances. To learn such self-control for the sake of performing great tasks is a common story theme. Through his own self-mastery, Saint George is given the power to pierce the dragon's throat and so to release the surrounding kingdoms from great suffering. All such stories have analogies in our own souls and bodies, where our forces may be held in captivity until discipline and right thinking be restored.

Create the story of a good cook who always knows what is needed and just how to prepare it. The enlightening concoctions of this cook may be surprising to a weary traveler at his or her inn or hearth.

Create a wicked but powerful cook who weakens the king and/ or queen through his evil designs. What punishment does this cook deserve when his plot is uncovered? Consider the royal rulers as aspects of yourself that need to be nourished with good will and wise choices.

MONSTERS AND GIANTS

Primitive story potentates and conflicts fuel our evolution to finer, wiser levels of existence. The great awkward strides, gestures, and appetites of these unwieldy monsters and giants awaken horror and compassionate humor. Their huge feet and hands are incapable of any refined activities; their hungers are gigantic. Giant wives are ever at the mercy of their husbands' needs for food and rest. When two giants or more meet in the old tales, they are weirdly slow and uncomprehending. They are always outwitted by the joyous cleverness of the quick-witted characters who meet them on the high-road and leave them safely behind in a jumble of awkwardness, perhaps even clubbing one another to death. They are usually pictured as living outdoors among great trees. Jack finds his giant atop a beanstalk wanting human blood for his dinner. In 'The Devil and the Three Golden Hairs' in the Grimm's collection, the giant is the devil down in hell. He too eventually is outwitted.

You contain a primitive gourmand which, like dragons of old, lives to eat, sleep, kill, and couple. Primal appetites want immediate gratification. They aim to absorb 'the blood of a Christian man' and any more advanced human quality that challenges their primitive nature. These primal appetites are rough drafts of evolving human greatness.

I wrote a story about a giant when I was unable to attend a great peace march, yet wanted to express my concern. I thought of the immense store of armaments in the world and the relatively diminutive peace initiative. I wondered what leaders and workers in armament factories might experience if they were confronted by this group of devoted peace lovers. 'What did Goliath feel about David?', I wondered. I took a pencil and let myself write. As I wrote, I became very purposive and collected, even though I had no idea how my story would unfold. I reread the description of Goliath in the Bible. 'Now it's a long way from here to there, and it's a long way back again', I began, 'but be that as it may.'

Yes, this was one of my authentic storytelling voices! 'There was once a boy called Goliath, and at first he was a boy no bigger than Bob or any of the big boys among us.' I thought I might have a chance to share the story at the school where I was teaching. 'His mother and father were away, gone to a conclave of giants. He was the youngest and they'd left him alone, to tend the goats.'

I gave my 'storyteller' full power. The sun was shining very brightly, and I knew I wanted the story to be a deed for peace. As I wrote, I kept shifting my position so that the sun was shining on my head and I could forget my dimmer self.

Goliath the giant boy stooped out of the dawn light into his family's hovel and found in its rafters and under the wooden floor the great weapons of his father. 'Out', he grunted, and he took them out; there was a great spear like a weaver's beam and the spearhead weighed 300 shekels of iron. There was a javelin of bronze, too, and he slung it between his shoulder blades.

Out he went, bonging his fat feet over the daisy heads. 'These are measley stars', he said, as he crushed their tiny white fairy eyes into the mud. Then he ate a bird raw, feathers and all. 'I'll get me a rabbit too', he growled. 'No, a buzzard. No, a bison. A wild bull. No, none of these is big enough for me. I'll jump the sun', he said; 'just wait till he's high as he gets. When he can get no higher, then I'll have him with all his foe – I'll get him down and have his ashes here in my hand. Then I'll hoe him into my father's garden.' He was a bit of a lunatic, this giant boy was.

So down he sat to wait for the sun to rise. And as he sat, his head fell over to one side and his shoulders fell down too, and then slowly his fatty eyelids fell down into the land of dreams. Up into his dreams came greasy monsters with red bones in their teeth and no kindness, and dancers without any form, and fighters with no stars in their eyes. But at last, too, in the farthest dim corner of his dream came a lank, lovely boy. 'No', groaned Goliath in his sleep.

The boy was golden with spirals of curls upon his head. And David came forth over the hills of Goliath's midsummer sleep. The arms of dream David were a golden lyre and his throat was all song. What he sang was warm and wise and stronger than death.

By this time I knew I wanted to finish the story. It was writing itself, and I was expressing my hope and belief that within every maker of armaments lives a deep yearning for peace.

Goliath vomited dead birds in his sleep. Then he rose up. His father's weapons lay all around him, horrible. And he longed for songs. His own throat was like a hoarse flu but now he had a craving for songs, and for the beauty of singing...

He wandered like a madman over the hills of Gath. And, when his father found him, he bound him in ropes and thwacked and thrashed him into oblivion so that the beautiful dream of the good beauty and peace fell away and wild, young Goliath forgot the new glory of the light.

When I had written the last paragraph, I felt I had a window into the heart of the armament makers of the world. If Goliath had accepted his own vision, could he have met David in another way? The process of writing the story helped me to feel the importance of cultivating my storytelling imagination to help me deal with what otherwise I could not understand.

Create a story in which three giants are overcome by a hero or heroine. Let the giants embody some of your worst fears about human nature. You can summon aid of any kind into your story world. What becomes of the giants after they have been outwitted or destroyed?

Tell the story of a giant child who lives in a giant's world but sometimes ventures out into places with normal dimensions.

Find similarities between modern armaments, prehistoric giant reptiles, and mythological giants. Pitch a group of wise children against all of these until they win.

GNOMES AND DWARFS

In many old stories and in your own story imagination you can find wily workers in the under-earth. These nature spirits do not like to be looked upon by ordinary human eyes. Always masculine in the old lore, they are fiercely protective and territorial. Usually night visitors to the human realm, they are capable of astonishing diligence in relation to the earth and its elemental substances. Their thoughts are keen and flashing, like cutting gemstones, and when aroused, they can be ruthless and destructive. Certain dwarfs have the power to cast extensive spells upon the stones and earth and also upon the visitors in their realms. Confined as these elemental beings are to the intense magnetic territories of the earth and responsible to them, nevertheless in stories they have been portrayed as longing for human contact and cooperation.

When the princess Snow White wanders into the mountain home of the dwarfs, they sense her pure and radiant human qualities and accept her into their protective circle. As a group these seven dwarfs experience the influences of the planetary spheres anchoring the influences of all the planets – Mars in the qualities of iron, Venus in copper, Saturn in lead. The snow white princess is like a perfectly transparent crystal of feminine human nature in their midst who reflects to them the promise of harmonious human love. Each gives his love to her as best he can until she grows to accept a truly human prince as her husband.

Dwarfs sometimes long to possess human beings as their own, like jewels, and so they must be outwitted. The lonely yearning of a dwarf-outcast is portrayed in the story of Rumplestiltskin – elemental alchemist, he possesses the power to spin ordinary matter into gold. His peculiar nature has mastered the desire for earthly gold, yet he must live apart, like an old hare or fox, longing for golden warmth of human love. When the queen has grown strong-willed enough to identify him, Rumplestiltskin disappears back into the earth.

You can let the gnarled, brilliant old protectors of the earth also find face and form in your stories where they may continue to manifest the power to transform and to help the earth and your own soul. Where you see the subtle interweaving of their substances with your own, let your characters become more courageous, clear, and awake like the Queen in 'Rumplestiltskin'.

Picture a gnome or group of gnomes as guardian of a piece of earth that you know and love. Let the character you imagine become very real to you. What do you think he would like you to know? Why doesn't he reveal himself?

Imagine a set of good dwarfs who are confused by human behavior and have retreated deep underground. What rituals might they devise in order to continue their work of protecting precious metals, stones, and 'ordinary' earth? Might they be interested in attracting extra-terrestrial helpers?

FAIRIES

Among many mysterious inhabitants of real and story landscapes are elementals called 'fairies' or 'devas' that encourage and defend the delicate lives of plants. Though modern minds may balk at them, there is no end to the tales that have explored and shall explore further the subtle interactions between the fairy and the human realms. Inaudible and invisible to our usual human eyes, these emissaries are especially of great interest to young children, 'real' without question until adult skepticism dispels them. Gathering around flowers, bushes, and trees, they sing and dance upward into the light. They can be found in the cascading morning light as the dews lift, and in the evenings, as petals fold. Some steady up sunbeams, perhaps to focus them on some neglected dump of sweet woodruff or violets. They dance in south winds, bringing warmth earthward to little sprouts. Rain fairies sprinkle dews and downpourings where they are needed most, holding off inclement moods of sky, channeling rain into neat puddles and streams. As snow and ice fairies, they collaborate with wintery weather to hold snow blankets over garden beds on deceptively warm days, and remind the seeds to sleep.

Fairy realms can be experienced as ominously attractive for whoever falls in love with their enchanting ways. Like sirens of the seas, they sometimes hold travelers too much in the sway of their transparent loveliness. Yet Ariel, Prospero's attendant fairy in Shakespeare's *The Tempest*, has the good fortune to have come into the power of a great human magician who understands him fully. Ariel wins new freedom through obedience to Prospero's human wisdom and good will.

Especially through story vision, you can experience the vast true story of earth's evolution. You have plant as well as animal nature within you. What you sing and say, how you move among birds and blossoms, leaves and spiraling tendrils – all your human gestures delicately intermix with the lives of plants. The reality of fairies lives within you. You, too, are a guardian and helper of sunlight, water, wind, and the circling seasons of the earth. You can welcome devas with assurance into your story realm and allow them to dance, sing, and work many wonders as you experience their need to commune with you.

I never heard of snow fairies when I was a girl, although I grew up in a part of New York State where snow piled up gigantically every winter. In my thirties when I went to live in England for a time, I met many people with subtle imaginations. After a time of puzzlement and bemusement, fairies began to feel somewhat real and possible to me too. A swirling place in my mind accepted them. I found numerous books in which they lived colorfully and convincingly. Eventually, the concept of 'fairy tales' took on new resonance and importance.

A young girl, who was staying at the hostel for children where I was working at that time, sewed some fairies out of delicate handkerchiefs. One morning I took one of these to the Waldorf kindergarten where I was storyteller. The English winter weather was mild by the standard I knew from my own childhood. Frost had covered the brown gorse bushes that were laced together with hundreds of beautiful spiderwebs. I felt the little lacey presence in my pocket, and I thought of the children's eager faces. As I walked to school, a story about a snow fairy was born. I didn't have to protect myself from snowball fights with my brothers and their friends. On the contrary, in this English atmosphere my relationship to the touch of cold was becoming more and more soulful and intricate. I wondered how my brothers might have felt about snow if we had had a living concept of fairies when we were children.

Suspend for a while your doubts about fairies. What might their real purposes be? Tell a story about a fairy or a group of fairies with a mission to protect a flower, a tree, or an airy territory from human destructive impulses.

Tell a story about a child who discovers an authentic fairy realm and how he or she protects this discovery.

ELVES

An elf has a flutelike airy presence, yet lives with its feet on the ground. Elves are playful earth-spirits that move with light-hearted glee in the human world, not unlike puppies or kittens but perhaps with higher intelligence and purpose. They are able to penetrate small openings in castles, houses, and barns. Because they lack the human pull of gravity underfoot, they sometimes cross the line into the fairy realm and sprout wings. Their shoes and hats tend to turn up with playful feathery lightness. Light-footed children with sweet, puckish features and slight relationship to gravity sometimes seem to have arisen out of their green elfish realms. Such children are able to identify with their antics in woodlands, meadows, and around old houses. Elves teach them their joyous elfin rhymes and rhythms.

In stories elfish speech is like sunlight and shadow, just as their pranks and hiding, secretive gift-giving and gift-receiving mirror the endlessly swift, surprising interrelationships that work in the brown and green shadows weaving within our natural surroundings. Deep in meadows, woodlands, and mansions of your heart, elves hide their subtle purposes. You can feel them yearning to come out and play, knowing they are ever-ready in the playful substance of your story imagination to make swift, joyous, witty mischief.

In the English countryside I began to feel many invisible presences. One spring day, inspired by the children's imaginations in the Waldorf School Kindergarten, I sewed a little elf. I didn't know exactly how his story would go. He came to school with me in my pocket. At the end of the morning, as a beginning storyteller, I sat down in the golden story chair while the children gathered around. The story was a surprise for me and the children; it began:

> *Not very far away, in the deep forest, lives an elf. Every morning when the sun comes up, he opens the doors of his hut and steps outside. His ears change their color and start to vibrate back and forth, and as he walks the nearby pathways, he listens for the creatures who need him. His ears are so large and fine and wide and full of kindness that they can hear even the tiniest voices of millipedes, ants, and turtles.*

This was an elf who would do no harm! In the process of making up this story, I was overcoming my fear of the ugly elves I had seen once in a picturebook when I was a child. I realized afterward that fear had cramped my elfin imagination at an early age.

> *One morning when he stepped outside very ear{J, he heard a very delicate sobbing coming from the center of the forest. His footsteps followed his ears – past big swaying beeches and oaks and old fallen logs – until he came to the one who was so sad. She was a small snow fairy, whose wings were impaled on the sharp thorns of a gorse busk. 'Poor snow fairy, what can I do for you?' asked this elf.*
>
> *'Can you free my wings please?' she sobbed angrily. 'All the others have flown off and left me here.' She felt too weak and outcast to notice the beauty of her prison.*
>
> *'Gorse bush's thorns have pierced your wings,' he said, 'but soon you will he free.' Then the elf expertly and carefully, began to extricate her*

wings. The gorse bush nodded to help. At last the elf succeeded. Then he lifted her down as gently as he could and wrapped her little wings into splints of oak shoots and feathers.

'Come with me far a spell. Soon you will be whole and well', he chanted to her. 'Just hold on to my ears', he said, when she was settled on his shoulders.

In my story the good elf brought her to his healing hut where he gave her the best of care. In the end she flew away on perfect wings. In other installments, this elf helped an old moth, a wounded field mouse, and several honeybees with early spring frostbite. I loved this story as it unfolded. Four years after I had told it, I met one of the children who had been in my kindergarten class. 'Do you remember the story about the elf?', she said with an almost-adult air and an astonishing smile. 'I'm not sure', I said. I had completely forgotten it. 'Can you help me remember?', I asked. 'Oh yes', she said, and took my hand! We sat on a bench and she recounted the story. I went home and wrote it out for her. She had a twin sister; their birthday was approaching, and she thought it would be a nice present for them to have from their former teacher. Having recently been suspended from school, an older student who had been wanting to do a good deed illustrated the story.

I felt grateful as another elf story occurred to me one day when I had been asked to help with a birthday celebration. An unusually joyful boy, about to turn six, was obsessed with 'ghost-busting'. Somewhat reluctantly, his parents wondered how they might use this theme for the party. They sensed that their noisy and otherwise fearless son was not happy about ghosts. The story began:

Once there lived in a little house a laughing, jolly, little man. Though he was small, he was fierce. His name was 'Pricklebeard-the-Laugher'. Mice scurried into their nests when he stepped out to stretch his little limbs in the morning light, spiders sped to the farthest corners of their webs when he passed by, and ants would stand at quiet attention or hurry away into their hills. Pricklebeard's feet were firm upon the earth wherever he went, and he was wont to sing loud songs at the top of his lungs...

So here was another powerful, benevolent elf! As I wrote, the frightened child I once had been breathed a sigh of relief deep within me.

One afternoon the skies were gathering heavy, grey clumps of clouds above the heads of all the trees. 'This is a fine day for bogles!', said the little man. Questing for ghosts was one of his pastimes. 'I will see what I can find.' Off he stomped toward the far town singing gloriously to himself till his little tongue shook. Soon be came to a red oak tree. 'Have you seen any ghosts today?'

Nodded the great oak, 'One passed this way very early, and disappeared over the hedge.'

'I will seek it', said Pricklebeard. So the elf sought bogles until he came to a castle that was full of them. 'I liberate ghosts', announced the little man proudly.

'You do?', fluttered a butterfly. 'Then you have much work to do!'

'Don't doubt me!', he shouted. 'You'll see!' and he shook his fist gleefully. A little man with a mission, he entered the silent castle in which was contained 'the largest collection of ghosts he had ever seen in one day'. Out of his pocket he drew his bogle-focus stone, and focused it first on one ghost, then on another. Men he had caught them all in the power of his crystal, he called out to all the royal folk who had been in hiding in the castle.

'Dear Pricklebeard, do you have them all?'

'With my trusty stone and all my heart', came his reply. Then up went a great hue and cry from all over the castle. Flags came out of the windows and flapped merrily in the breezes. 'Pricklebeard the Liberator!' He was laughing loudly. 'Pricklebeard-the-Laugher!'

Just then the sun broke through a dark cloud at the horizon. Long, beautiful fingers of sunlight reached through the skies beyond the castle. A great feast was set out. 'Hurrah far Pricklebeard-the-Liberator!'

After dinner the owl perched on the high castle wall to help complete the liberation, should his help be needed. One by one, as the King and Queen and all the royal family and guests watched, the Liberator of Ghosts turned his stone in the firelight. First one ghost shot out of the crystal and into the darkening skies. They watched it go up, toward the starlight and disappear. Then another went. And another, each one guided up and away by the knowing owl.

'Where are they going?', asked a Princess.

'To the other side of the Sun where their journey was begun', shouted Pricklebeard. As each ghost was released, he wildly somersaulted and so did some of the royal children.

'Are the ghosts afraid to go so far?', she asked.

'The owl helps them see their way out. They don't like being ghosts, but they are afraid to go out there where they can be new-made and turn into better human beings.' After some more festivities Pricklebeard's liberating stone was empty of ghosts. 'A good day's work done!' ,he shouted merrily, though truly he was feeling a little tired. But before they all went to bed, the royal children made him promise that they could help him in the future.

'Indeed', he said. And from that day on, when it was Ghost-Liberating Day, Pricklebeard and his royal friends and the owl found and liberated many bogle-ghosts of many kinds until there were no more to be found in all that land. And then they were happy remembering, and told stories in the castle of their exploits and adventures with the Laugher and the Liberator – Pricklebeard-the-Great.

All the birthday guests received crystals as party favors. Led by the young host, delightful and satisfactory 'ghost-liberating' activities took place during the birthday party, that ended with a great releasing of white and silver helium balloons. The story had brought his imagination into control and everyone was happy. The real-life elf's older sister beautifully illustrated the story in a book which was given to him after the party was over.

Imagine a house near a woodland and populate it with a helping or a mischievous elf who interacts with the human family that lives there.

Model out of clay or wax a story-elf that can sit on an empty book. Gradually fill the story-elf's book with little rhymes and stories. Let these be for a child you know and for the very real child who lives within you. An inspiring book about elves is Isabel Wyatt's *The Seven Year Wonder Book*.

ANGELS

At boundaries and danger-points in your stories, and in real life, quite suddenly helpers and healers can appear. Those who accept them into their lives are helped to go on cheerily, merrily, strengthened, or calmed, perhaps healed of deep wounds or woes. Those who reject these mysteriously beneficent helpers – in storyland, as in life – must go on suffering, creating their downward course. Although not always beautiful and winged, these presences graciously offer a way out of trouble. Self-effacing though they may be, they often speak wise counsel. An angel may take the appearance of a wandering sage with a tangled beard, a wise woman muffled in cape and boots, a gardener at work tending roses or whitethorn, a blind cowherder, or a shining little shepherd girl.

As in the tales of George MacDonald, the helper may be peacefully settled into a healer's hut in deep woodland, wearing a beautiful green robe, or into an upper chamber where she is spinning the threads of her beloved child in everlasting moonlight. In other stories an angelic guardian may be disguised in the unattractive form of a beggar or of an idiot child. In 'Snow White and Rose Red' the children who fall asleep at the edge of a precipice are protected all through the night by a child dressed in white. Sometimes a discarnate host can appear in the form of flocking birds or marvelously singing winds. What these angels-in-disguise have in common, whether loathsome, gracious, human, or discarnate, is their immense good will toward the wandering one at the center of the story. If their secret be withheld until a spell of work has been completed to perfection, or their talisman or other 'magic' will only work under certain circumstances, the help nonetheless shall be exactly what is needed.

Robert, an unusually kind and thoughtful father, wrote a story called 'A Rocking Chair Day'. It began with a description of the life of a young man who was consumed with work and partying.

One Sunday morning as he sat rocking, it was 'as if I were being whispered to'. Next day, opening his eyes, he felt struck as if by a lightning bolt at how differently the world looked. Questions began.

Friends who enjoyed a camaraderie through the grape could not stand the transforming soul and faded in the coming months and years. Have you ever been sober at a party where everyone else was not? A presence, till then unperceived, entered my journey and we went the different way.

A woman on a grueling story journey came to a series of rapids on her story-donkey. She wondered how to get the creature as well as herself across them. She went to the riverbank and wished for help. Suddenly she saw a small, gnarled creature appear with a golden rope in its hands. It asked her what she wanted. She told it she wanted to get across. It said it would help her.

Breathe great kindness and care in and out slowly twelve times. Listen to your breaths as if they were wing beats.

Tell the story of a true mysterious intervention in your own life. To re-experience this presence you may wish to ask a partner or several others to act out your story with you.

Tell a story about one or two children who set out on a journey and are lost. Let three dangers be met. See that the children are guided safely on each time by guardian presences.

CREATURE COMPANIONS

In your own stories, you can experience the qualities of animals as aspects of yourself. Every animal, insect, and bird offers energy to us: the diligence of a bee gathering sweetness for its queen, a bird's lightness and swiftness, a tiger's rippling power, a peacock's grandeur. Creatures that accompany story characters can also be pictures of qualities or energies that we want to transform. A venomous snake, a yapping bitch, or irritatingly libidinous old goat may follow behind a character for a time, finally to disappear into the mists or badlands of the tale or to be swiftly and mysteriously redeemed. A snake skin that has been cast off may have the power to heal when the princess picks it up. The bitch may frighten away worse creatures than she is with her endless yap. The goat may rise into the zodiacal stars of Capricorn and from above throw down its challenges to the libidinous king.

Creatures sometimes accompany characters throughout their adventures, as totems. A lone wolf inspires an American Indian child to imitate its ingenious powers of survival. The cat teaches the princess its ancient power of insight and inwardness. Fox children teach a maiden swift and delicate movements for dangerous moments in dark places. An owl awakens the powers of a nightwatcher who must overcome sloth and ordinary sleep to enter into the truth of dreams. In some tales creatures find a sort of human voice; what the creature says may be decisive as the adventurer moves on. To set creature-talk apart from the human world, their communications are often spoken in rhymed verse, unique vocabulary, or odd syntax. The rhymed commands of the grey wolf in 'The Firebird' saved the prince again and again on his journey to true love and enlightenment.

In other stories and in the stories you yourself tell and write, an elusive creature may be portrayed, disappearing ahead of a character, representing a future task or encounter that will occur when the time is right and certain conditions have been met. Perhaps it is a visionary bird, as it was for Hansel and Gretel, that sometimes sang to help them find their way through the witch's forest. True love may be waiting where the creature lives – someone having sent it out from his or her heart's desire as emissary or scout. In the fabulous tale 'The Two Brothers', collected by the Brothers Grimm, a parade of loyal, delightful beasts goes with the twins, like angels, to help them when their human powers are not enough to meet the dire events they have to face.

In reality, great willingness to serve our human world lives in the animal kingdoms, provided we are willing to serve them too. It is important and satisfying to contemplate this interweaving mutuality of the human and animal worlds through story imagination. What gives creatures the power to help is often, in stories as in life, the care and attention that has come from a human being. By deep laws of cause and effect, whoever ignores their needs suffers accordingly. In 'The Queen of the Bees', the queen bee herself tells the gentle Simpleton how he and his more careless brothers may be saved from becoming stone statues in a lifeless garden. Animal helpers are likewise thoughts and deeds that return to us in difficult times, giving us the power to see our way and to persevere. By a mysterious process, kind deeds return to the doer. In stories this delicate process that weaves through every life is portrayed in ways which we can scarcely grasp with our rational minds.

You have within your heart a tender flame for the needs of all living things. From this heart's light you are able to notice the adventures and adversities of even the tiniest creatures. Your story self is filled with creatures of all sizes, shapes, and dispositions that sometimes are eager to serve the needs of human characters. You grow more and more attentive to their creature qualities and needs as you recognize their willingness to give wisdom and help in your story world, and to accompany, with their marvelous characteristics, your story characters, to help and support them on their way.

I had been feeling sad for weeks and thought to myself, 'I have stopped singing'. I wondered if I might write a story that would illuminate the reason. I had often written stories for others, but now I wanted to try my own medicine. I gave myself an hour and sat down with a pencil and some scraps of used paper, remembering that most of my best writing has been done when I have been out of sorts with myself and unable to reason my way into a happier outlook. When I finished this story, I knew in my bones about the weird dark power inside me and others that tries to destroy beauty and to banish love. I have read my story to myself many times to remind me of its truth. In my story a girl was turned into a parrot whose voice was muffled among many other enchanted birds by a horrid witch. A blind man knew about the witch's house.

The witch saw him leaning against the far corner of the house, in a ray of sun. Quickly she put him to work as guard to her birds. Whenever the witch was indoors, he held the nearest cage to his heart, and wept. Toward the end of the day the deer came to the edge of the witch's clearing. The blind man mounted the deer and disappeared among the trees.

Not many days and nights had passed before the blind man returned with the deer in the moonlight. With him came water from an ancient spring. Having dug very deeply where the deer had taken him, the blind man made a runnel for the water to follow through the woods. The water was singing softly. Wherever the deer stepped in the moonlight, the man felt his way and dug his trench further. Before the witch was awake, around her whole house had flowed a ringing moat that was full of the singing waters. At dawn she heard the sound of the waters and was filled with fear. She clawed at the bed-covers. Bitterness and confusion gathered in a gall at her belly; hatred cramped her heart. She closed her ears with her thumbs. The sound of the beautiful water flowed through windows and walls. She dared not scream for fear of awakening her birds to even worse sounds by the power of imitation. At last she fled to a secret chamber under the earth and concealed herself down there.

The deer stood luminously at the door. The blind man opened it. When he found the old witch-mother in her hiding place, he dragged her out into the open and put her into a large cage he had made for her beside the singing water. There she had to crouch. The deer stood guard. Then the blind man entered the house and began to feel his way to the squelched birds. For him each of their cages was a knot to untie, a snarl to unravel. He grasped them one by one with his sensitive hands. He felt in them the witch's raging fear of beauty.

At the end of this story, after all this powerful feminine energy had been liberated, 'the deer stood at the flowing water's edge, a motionless sentinel' and the witch lay dead at the bottom of her cage. I was completely amazed by the imagery I had produced, simply because I had set myself the task to write myself out of my misery. The white deer, as angelic sentinel, appeared in another part of the same woods in a story I wrote some weeks later.

Create a character in deep distress and let an animal come to his or her aid. Set your imagination free to visualize this helping creature. Whether it speaks in rhymes or is silent, let it tell you about a quality that helps you deal with adversity in your own life and in the lives of others. Let the creature see what the humans cannot yet see or have forgotten how to see.

Create a delightful parade of creatures that accompany a child as he or she sets out into the world. How does each of these creatures help the child out of difficulties?

DRAGONS AND MYTHICAL BEASTS

Deep in the evolutionary folds of your brain dreams a 'reptilian brain'. Stories can take you very close to the breath of this primeval beast, that sends its long tail down into the sheathe of every human nerve cord. It sometimes rouses from sleep in the ancient lairs of our bones. As we accept 'dragons' and other primeval reptiles into our story terrain, so as better to comprehend their powers, habits, and needs, we can learn to harness their fire and longevity and fabulous periodic hungers. In traditional dragon stories, a conqueror arrives just in time with fortitude and courage enough to subdue the dragon. Then, the pure and noble maiden triumphantly returns to the town with her hero, the beast quelled in between or just behind them – or dead. We may see every aspect of the story as ourselves. At times we seem in mortal danger of being consumed by the fires of our hunger, thirst, and lusts, about to be sacrificed to the fabulous brute forces in our natures, to diabolic designs, to entropy; yet, the soul forces we have developed through long aeons allow us to rise above these. The archetypal dragon tale with its many permutations helps us to see ourselves as beast, maiden, and saintly warrior and to bring these again and again into order, celebration, and harmony.

Unicorns appear, pure and white, from the depths of forests and meadows. These beasts wait to be tamed by the loving touch of a human maiden. A unicorn that has been lovingly tamed no longer impels hunters to torment and kill it. Found and loved by a beautiful maiden, the unicorn may offer its mysterious energies and powers to all who truly honor it.

Fire-birds and other high-flyers of story-lore remind us of the sublime heights into which we can soar – especially at night or in our daydream consciousness – when we feel liberty from flesh and earthly gravity. These visionary birds of the royal gardens of our souls rise and perch in beautiful trees beyond ordinary grasp. Tsar Vyslav Andronovich of the Russian tale 'The Firebird' offers all his kingdom to the one who can bring down this elusive luminosity for him. Only the son who is most graced with discipline and heart can bring it to his father intact and alive, together with the great mystery of true love found. The bird, an angelic force, motivates the coming of a new order in the kingdom.

Dragons embody fiery primeval hungers; unicorns, the wild need for loving touch. Dragon, unicorn, and fire-bird-phoenix all illuminate the 'old order'. In the drama of their wise subjugation, new realms of joyous love and wisdom come into being from your own efforts to understand them and to evolve. Again and again you can discover blueprints for wise rulership through the archetypal pictures that are offered in story-lore.

Autumn is dragon season. Trees seem to be on fire; there is breath of ash and burning in the air. To waken the tremendous fires within us, to unleash them, might eat up or burn up all that is civilized. Yet we know that dragon-fire threatens us continually. Children, especially those with a fiery nature, sometimes feel themselves to be in the grip of a dragon. They move powerfully and impulsively, knocking into people and furniture. When children are in this fire-breathing mood and not feeling very sympathetic to the 'maiden', we can intensify the fires for them. The adventures of a hero, with strength, courage, and charity, help them to transform their wild energy.

A dragon story for a child who is more connected with the air, by contrast, might present many light details. The colors of the dragon, the birds flying by that get their feathers singed, and the exact insects and flowers that were burned by its breath, might well interest them. Not so much the inner strength of the hero, but descriptions of his hat and sword and jewels are what these children want to hear. Name the jewels and tell their size and weight and where they are from: they will welcome your digressions. Less fire and blood will be needed. At the end of this kind of tale the maiden and hero might collect colorful scales and teeth from the dragon to keep sentimentally in a jeweled box.

In a more melancholy mood, you might conjure an old dragon who has been around for ever and a day. Only an old man, perhaps with one eye, had seen this dragon long ago. Or maybe a little boy hasn't slept for weeks because he was having bad dreams about it. It may be a pathetic creature, with his teeth fallen out, who comes out only when it is particularly safe to hiss sadly. Melancholic children, and melancholics who have grown up, often feel tired; they are especially tired of their incessant, compulsive brooding, yet they can possess deeply heroic souls. Like Hamlet, they think about grand and glorious deeds but have difficulty carrying them through. The dream-sword of St Michael or of Saint George vanished, yet the wise father in the story says: 'It's true. The gift of the dream sword is real – you can do a fine deed with this inner power.' This sort of child can appreciate a serious significance for a sword. In his story the boy may give his sword to one who is strong and active, lending his thoughts and understanding to the other's strength of heart and hand.

A story for a slow and dozy child might center around a cuddly dragon sleeping under the porch. A child pokes at the little dragon with a rake. He goes to get a friend who pokes at it. Phlegmatics enjoy repetition. They get grandmother – they may get seven or seventeen people to come. Accumulation is important. Getting more peas, more potatoes, more and more of anything characterizes phlegmatic souls. Finally this dragon wakes up and is hungry! What does it enjoy eating? One by one, each person brings what he thinks the dragon would like to eat. Inside, the grandmother is making a pie. She brings it out and offers it to the dragon. The baby dragon becomes the household darling. Then, this dragon lifts its wings and is briefly able to fly around the room, up the stairwell, and back down before returning to its quiet, autumnal nest.

Styling a dragon to the mood of young children can also be helpful to adults, who want to relate to an 'inner child.'

In detail imagine a dragon that is holding an individual, a family, or a whole town in terror. Create a hero or heroine, or both together, who meet this dragon and successfully absorb its power as their own, putting its power compassionately and cleverly in the service of others.

Tell a dragon story to yourself as a child, allowing the dragon to express your own mood and needs.

Write and illustrate a story about a unicorn in which a hero or heroine has lost his or her sense of touch and has become numb to the surroundings – finding the unicorn transforms their lives.

Tell a story about a beautiful fire-bird that longs to be seen and accepted by human beings. Whenever the fire-bird is near in your story you might add musical touches with a stringed instrument such as a lyre.

BIRDS

Birds can fly into your stories, bringing a sense of upliftment and airy freedom. When the white pigeons and turtle-doves, 'and at last all the birds beneath the sky' come to Cinderella through the open kitchen window, they alight in the ashes to help her find the good grains that her stepmother had thrown there for her to pick up. They are kin to the bird-spirit that lives in the tree, which Cinderella planted at her mother's graveside. Whatever she wishes for, this white bird of loving protection throws it down to her.

When birds come into a story as helpers, they can also solve riddles and mysteries and sing about what must be done. Like angelic visitors, they see and speak beyond the power of available human sight and speech. In the strange story 'The Three Languages' in the Grimm's collection, an 'unteachable' count's son is able to learn the language of birds from an enlightened master. To the old count this power of inner listening is of no account, yet at the end of the story, the youth who has learned to listen is able to become a high priest and to speak the pure wisdom his bird guides sing into his ears. Siegfried also heard the language of the birds after dragon's blood had been sprinkled on his tongue; how what is heard is comprehended makes the story unfold in its special way. American Indian heroes and heroines feel the falcon or eagle feather-spirit penetrating upward from head or back toward the heights from which it had fallen down; the bird's wide vision, swift flight, and sure sense of direction become part of their own nature as they venture forth for the sake of their people.

Birds carry different qualities into stories. Owl-eyes stay open for long periods of time with a strangely human and golden look. Perched on the trees of storyland, they may represent the climb we make through the branches of our own bodies and minds that so often seem in the dark, like trees in a night forest. The 'owl' sees even in the depths of night, and like a spiritual leader offers wise advice from its height in a story's tree. Eagles also offer majesty of wing and breadth of view; having the ability to soar higher and see farther than any other winged creature, the eagle is emblematic of the closest companion of Jesus, Saint John. His vision closes the New Testament in the book called Revelation. So in the story world of imagination, apocryphal wisdom may pour through a story bird that knows from the heights the ways of the earth and can bring far-seeing vision down to earth.

Invite the benevolence of birds into your story world. Their beautiful movements, penetrating vision in the day and the night, their diligence, and their singing voices connect them with the angelic realms above your story characters. You nest within your own body and mind 'all the birds beneath the sky' by the power of your imagination. You can find these winged creatures within you as pictures of the whirring wisdom you need, that your inner vision and your stories also may fly.

A mathematician in her fifties complained that she had no creativity. One evening I invited the small group she had joined to write a story in which someone who is held in confinement, like a seed, finds a way to the light. Everyone wrote for about an hour without stopping, feeding on the creative energy of the group as they sat in growing twilight around a candle with music playing quietly in the adjoining room. Here is the first part of the story that she wrote:

Penelope was curled up asleep in a dark earthen den. She had been there, it seemed, for a long time. She would awake, and sensing that nothing had changed, she would return to sleep. She was wrapped in her long, golden hair.

She heard a tapping that brought her to consciousness. She looked around and saw nothing; she continued to hear the sound. Since she couldn't see its origin, she got to her knees. She couldn't stand; the space was too small. 'How long have I been here?', she thought. The tapping grew louder. She imagined that something was breaking through the wall of her cavern. She located the source of the sound and stared in that direction. It was so gloomy that it was hard to see. Finally she saw a speck of green against the brownish wall ahead of her.

As time passed, she saw that it seemed to be a beak – the head of a green bird, a large green bird. The bird broke through the wall, spread its wings, and enveloped her. Strange to say she didn't feel fear but comfort. She could feel the strong beat of the bird's heart. It rose up with her and pushed through the top of the cavern. They emerged into a larger space that had an underground river and a waterfall.

This was the beginning of a journey during which Penelope was followed at every step by the benevolent presence of the green bird. The energy and courage Glennette received from writing this story seemed sadly evanescent to her, even though she did read her story to a number of her friends. Yet, when she sat down to write another imaginative journey, she had more confidence in herself. Her visual imagination, so clear and vivid, was leading her into a new sense of movement and trust in herself and others. When she went home to visit her old mother after these writing experiences, she decided that she would not curl herself away and read books as much as she habitually did, but would take more pleasure in relating to herself and her mother and sister.

In a story I wrote for a friend who was feverish and congested on her birthday, much to my surprise, a tigress took flight.

After a time of turning and whirling, the tigress pounced down on her soft paws, shining exuberantly, joyously. 'I will fly you wherever you wish to go.'

'Fly me to air that dances', cried Felina. 'Fly me to winds that sing.'

The tigress flew them straight ahead through jungle heat for a long while, until at last Felina, when she looked down beneath her, saw great trees were dancing. But the tigress, who did not have human ears, did not hear the beautiful singing that Felina heard.

As the story went on, with the helping power of the winged tigress, Felina sang and danced. My friend thanked me but said she did not like the story. I tell this here because, of course, not all story medicine works.

My basketful of archetypal puppets is guarded by a white bird with large outspread wings. The wings move by the blue strings that are attached to its wing-tips. Though created haphazardly one morning before I rushed off to school, since then it has been brought into many stories. When it is not simply watching, countless times it has carried two and sometimes more to adventure and to safety and peace.

Imagine a bird that embodies peace, joy, kindness, happiness, or any other qualities. Let your protagonist be caught in a blank place or other dilemma where there seems to be no help, and allow the bird to come willingly to serve, uplift, and protect her and others.

In an otherwise dark story, let an owl see very plainly what is needed.

Cast a tight place into a story. This may be an area of your own life, which you recognize is squeezed, where you have lost your sense of perspective. Your own home or office sometimes might feel like a tangled briar-patch or dull hollow. In your story let a brilliantly colored eagle soar above this confusion and throw down useful items and messages out of the blue.

HORSES

Horses in myth and in fairy-tale lore provide power and grace. With a swoop and bounding leap they can even carry you into divine ideas. The Greeks pictured Pegasus as the pure white moving force that could carry poetic nature to the stars on its great and willing wings, balancing through vast cosmic rhythms. In 'Faithful Ferdinand' a child is born to two poor people who cannot find a godfather for him until a stranger in a church gives them a key, which is to be kept safe until the boy reaches his fourteenth year. Then the boy finds the castle to which the key fits and in it a white horse. The horse tells the young man what he needs to know and to ask for in order to survive the trials set for him. As he overcomes each hurdle, the horse acts as his cosmic helper until the young man is able to create an orderly, loving kingdom in which to live. Similar to this is the horse of the king's daughter, named Falada, in 'The Goose-girl'. Falada can speak and is a most faithful and loyal companion throughout the girl's terrible trials.

In the Book of Revelation, the four apocalyptic horses are bathed in colors. The white horse of purest spiritual wisdom and guidance gives way to a red horse of passion and egoism, to a black horse carrying scales of judgment and dissection. The fourth horse is 'pale', its rider is

Death. Whatever color a story horse may be, it carries us far into realms of truth. The Rosicrucians favored the image of a grey horse moving between the light and the dark, blending both into misty light from which at any moment might spring out the full spectrum of colors.

In your stories, a rider you invent may change from horse to horse as he or she moves through different inner landscapes, taking on various colors and qualities. Horses that have affinities with the light and with the dark may carry a rider on a wise or a confused or destructive route with upward flights or downward plunges. Story horses have warmth, flaring nostrils, flowing musculature that jet planes, at their best, cannot express. Their trembling warm eagerness, gentle cooperation, intelligence, and beauty add power, dash and sometimes measureless heights, depth, and distance to what otherwise might be an ordinary adventure.

Include the carrying strength of a horse among your story creatures, for often you may need this quality as you progress through your story landscapes. Like the donkey in 'The Strange Musician', you have within you the power to move through awkwardness and limitation to joyously graceful, companionable strengths.

Think of a quality that you feel is quite immobilized or ineffectual in your personal life, and picture it as characteristic of the protagonist whom you describe and name at the start of your story. Present your protagonist with a magnificent horse on which he/she may ride toward your true goals. Perhaps your horse will also have the power of speech and of humble and most patient self-sacrifice. Throughout your story it will help you to reach your goals in surprising ways, no matter how difficult the obstacles that must be met.

Take a story journey on a great white-winged steed.

FOXES AND WOLVES

Animals represent ancient words in the symbol language of fairy stories – each with its different slant of meaning. A fox, like a rat, may indicate cleverness, silent observation, and the ability to run through thicket and stronghold. Too wily and swift to be easily caught in any snare, it can patiently wait and observe with a relentless ability to outwit dimmer faculties and to get its own way, feeding its appetites successfully to its own satisfaction. In the Middle Ages, the devil was sometimes pictured as an upright, speaking fox.

Wolves also have oftentimes taken on a villainous image – dark, rapacious, relentless, like the power of darkness that consumes life and light in its mighty grasp. The ancient Persians pictured death as a wolf. The fragile, innocent self setting out through the great forest of life, as Red Ridinghood on her mission to bring health to the old, ill 'grandmother', is consumed in the wolf's belly. Story imagination has sometimes designated 'wolf' to mean destructive science; crude desire for sex, money, or things; disbelief; despair whatever consumes our ability to foster wellbeing.

When the god Wotan of the Niebelungenlied fathered a race of humans who could have free will, he called these offspring 'wolflings' and clothed them in wolf skins. Each human 'wolfling' has to experience rapacious wolflike desires in order to develop freedom of choice. In the founding of vast domains of Rome, this myth developed further in the tale of Romulus and Remus who were said to have been suckled by a she-wolf and so received her qualities and passed them on to all the realm. Tales such as 'The Wolf and the Seven Little Kids' of the Grimm's collection show that rescue comes from the consuming power of 'the wolf'. The little goat in the ticking clock knows the true story of the wolf's designs on its brothers and sisters and can tell it. The loving mother goat and the observant, ready woodsman liberate them, and the little kids come back to life much wiser than they were.

Positive pictures of wolves arise also as the mysterious boundaries between the animal and human world shift and play in stories, such as in the Russian tale of 'The Firebird'. In that story, a prince, having lost his grey horse, ventures through dark fields on the back of a grey wolf. As he searches for the phoenix bird, the wolf penetrates forests and darkness with powers unfamiliar to the boy. Similarly the totem-power of wolf among certain American Indian tribes, recognition and acceptance of the mysterious helping energies of the creature, allow them to reach their human goals. In 'The Firebird' the wolf is a human in disguise who, when all the trials are met, can resume a fully human form. In such stories animals are already very close to being human but must do good deeds and win the cooperation of human beings in order to go free from their merely animal bodies. They have been longing to give their services to human souls willing to work with them.

Through stories you can nurture your connections with creatures whose qualities enhance your own. You can experience intimately through your imagination the yearning to be free from the limitations of mere animal nature. As you focus compassionately, you can awaken your capacity to transform the dominating wiles of your animal-like nature into generous, potent human love.

When a teacher had to leave a group of young children who loved her, I was privileged to be asked to make up and tell a story that would help her and the children to say goodbye to one another. Whenever I begin to create a story to ease a situation, I am aware of much more than I have gathered to make the story work out well. Somehow the children were with me and their parents behind them as well as the good will of the other teachers. The image of this teacher's spiritual master also came before me. The teacher loves foxes and the image of a fox-maiden leapt into my heart. I imagined that in the daytime she roamed freely as a fox, and at night she threw off her fox-fur and became the guardian of children who had ventured so far out into the forest that they could not find their way home without her help. The more I wrote, the more inspired and content I became. When I came to the end of the story, I knew that it would be medicine, because my intuition had been successfully tapped, as if little bells were ringing. I carefully wrote out the story and made a book of it so that the children would enjoy seeing me turn its pages and so that their teacher could have it as a keepsake. When I told 'Fox-furs', she laughed and wept openly with the children and they were all very close. As a gift to the children and as her final parting gesture to the school, that summer the teacher wrote a beautiful story herself. Since then she has written and told many wonderful stories to help troubled children.

An unusually gentle man discovered a wolflike monster in one of his stories. This snout-nosed beast lurked in a castle. It lured a three-year-old child on to a rampart and there ate out the child's throat until it died.

This vividly tragic event in his imagination preoccupied the man. He felt the helplessness and terror of the child in his story and, stimulated by its plight, brooded on many questions. Only after several months did a realization dawn. Deadly terrors often grip the throats of children. Within his story he could go further. Like the creator of 'The Juniper Tree', his dead child could come to life again and grow whole. A golden bird could sing the truth to everyone. The beast could be transformed.

Tell the story of an enchanted wolf that is reluctant to become a man, resists transformation again and again, and yet again until at last he submits to disenchantment and finds he has become, perhaps despite himself, older and wiser.

Retell the story of Little Red Riding Hood in your own terms. What is the most destructive habit you know of, that can eat you up completely? Set an innocent child, your own 'inner child', on a path through dark woods to bring medicine of bread and wine to your wise old grandmother self. Tell how your child is drawn off the path by this dark distraction. At the end of your story the good-hearted 'woodcutter', who symbolizes your insight and sense of inner direction, will have to liberate your child and wise old self.

CATS

The whole cat family is your kin, and you are kin to them. You have only to invoke your own feline powers and to allow them to play in your story imagination. The lion's roar and lung capacity far surpass ordinary human powers. Its penetrating vision also may surpass ours. When a lion or lioness finds the way into human insight and speech, great golden truths mysteriously may emerge from their mouths, shifting the boundary between animal and human. In 'The Twelve Huntresses', a king's pet lion speaks truths no human being will admit to.

'The Two Brothers' portrays two young guardian lions that follow and protect the twin human brothers, speak the truth and give wise commands. One of them returns the head to his master's broken body the wrong way around, but quickly repairs his mistake. He also knows how to knock on the king's door with his tail and how to bear wine to his master, carrying the basket handle in his mouth. As a staunch shining servant in the story, he wears the 'golden clasp' of his master's true love until he becomes a man and is able to marry her.

The breathing power of a magical lion or lioness may allow it access to deep and powerful expressions of feeling, as the great deeds and utterances of the holy lion Aslan in *The Chronicles of Narnia*, by C. S. Lewis. Traditional symbology can guide our story pictures today. In Christian iconography the lion, which is associated with the Gospel of Saint Mark in the New Testament, balances with the symbols of bull, eagle, and man that represent the other three gospels. In story language, lion, bull, and eagle each bring unique gifts of feeling, willing, and seeing.

Smaller representatives of the cat family also find their way into story creations. The quietness, gracefulness, and cleanliness of the whole cat family inspire admiration. Cats are able to live in crypts and temples as guardian spirits to the dead. If their voices and gestures can be understood in the safe confines of a story, they can impart much wisdom from those netherworlds. An otherwise unassuming cat wears boots that take it on huge journeys in a few moments in 'Puss-in-Boots'. In 'The Fox and the Cat' the cat is able, unlike the proud fox, to protect herself completely from dogs.

A school counselor set out to make a story for a six-year-old who was having trouble at home and at school. She cast his problems into imaginative pictures.

Dalgha seldom saw his father, the King, because he was often away in foreign lands with his army. Dalgha's father had given him the important and mysterious task of carrying his favorite object back and forth across the city every day to his grandmother's house. No ordinary flower vase, it was made of crystal glass and blown in the shape of a lion. When the sun fell upon it, the lion's eyes would twinkle with light and his mane would shimmer with a thousand colored rainbows. It was a majestic crystal lion, and Dalgha loved it almost as much as his father did. So every day he did as his father asked and took the lion vase through the streets of the Great City.

In the course of this story, the boy drops the lion and it shatters into a million pieces. This tragic accident, however, puts him in contact with a wise and powerful old shopkeeper who changes the glass first into gold and then, after the boy has become more generous and courageous at school, back into a perfect transparent lion. Because they sensed it was special, the kindergarten children listened together to the long story of the glass lion with very deep attention.

Although giving story medicine can sometimes disrupt usual procedures, it also changes behavior very effectually, especially when the story pictures are accepted by both adults and children and brought back to the children's awareness carefully for a number of days. Fortunately, however, this is not always necessary; some medicine is hungered for so deeply and is so lovingly administered, as happened in this case, that one good dose is enough.

Create a story about a pet lion or lioness that, when it opens its mouth, always roars out the truth.

Create a Halloween story in which a wise little cat who lives in a cemetery or underground temple guards the spirits of the dead. Let this creature come into the dreams of children and calm their fears with whiskered dignity.

Let a lion, a bull, and an eagle bring strength and healing to a lonely figure who has to cross difficult terrain.

BEES, ANTS, AND OTHER INSECTS

Both the ants and the bees present pictures of astonishing co-operation, order, and industry. Minds, like honey hives, store life's sweets in orderly patterns and like ant kingdoms, build inner realms with many chambers and passageways. In 'The Queen of the Bees' Simpleton demands that his brothers leave in peace the creatures that they would have disturbed for their amusement and pleasure. So, by the mysterious laws of relationship, when Simpleton is in danger of losing his own life, tiny creatures come to help him survive, calling out to him from the earth, the air, and the water. The king of the ants commands his fellow workers to scurry and gather together no less than the pearls of his true love. Then the queen of the bees herself helps him truly to recognize the love of his life, so that he may awaken her, with all her realm, to new life.

The active wisdom at work in such tiny, sociable creatures can bring great joy to any story realm. The sociable patterns of bees and ants awaken trust in the wise patterns weaving in all things. As you honor and protect small creatures in their own realms, their wisdom can come directly to us and to our story characters who are seeking to live in harmony and balance with themselves and others.

More ants had moved into my house than I could put out the kitchen door. At that time 'The Queen of the Bees' had become one of my favorite stories. Early in the morning as I sat having my breakfast, I saw the queen of the ant nest lumbering with great dignity across the kitchen floor. My first impulse was to squash her, yet in a flash I was inspired by the story of Simpleton's relationship with the ants in the fairy tale. I went down on my hands and knees to this queen ant, bowing my head all the way to the floor. With sincerity and courtesy that surprised me, I heard myself saying: 'O great queen, I have admired your people for a long time. But now I have a request. Could you please lead them all out of my place.' I told her about the beauty of the backyard. I said I didn't want to harm even one of her kind but that there were so many of them and they were showing me no respect. To my great surprise, we seemed to have understood one another enough, for not one ant did I ever have in my kitchen again for the three succeeding years I lived in that place.

Another story touched me deeply and further changed my relationship with insects.

A great saint, Columba, lived long ago on the island of Iona in Scotland. In one of the many tales told of his life, he was said to have gone to pray in his cell for three days and three nights, not to be disturbed by anyone. Yet, a large black fly would not leave his cell. After two days and two nights of its continuous buzzing, the saint lost his patience, shouting, 'Art thou a thing from hell?'. By this shout, his ears were opened, and he could understand the voice of the fly.

'You have given your blessing to all the four-footed creatures of this isle', the fly complained. 'You have blessed the fishes and creatures of

the sea. You have blessed the winged birds, but you have not blessed the winged insects, and I am one.'

When Columba heard this he immediately summoned all the holy brothers of the monastery. Gathering into a circle by the side of the sea, together they offered prayers and blessings for the flies and all the winged insects of that island. From that day on Columba and his brothers had command of the insects and lived in harmony with them.

Many times this story has inspired me to speak firmly with a blessing to mosquitos and flies. I have more often than not found that they 'listen'. As they fly out the door or window, I say, 'You will like it much better out there. Please tell your relatives not to come here. Thank you!'

Tell a story of a bee as if this little creature is a part of yourself and knows how to gather exactly what it needs even if pollen is sparse.

Tell a story in which insects communicate their needs. Let them speak to human beings who are willing to listen to their requests and to honor them.

SNAKES

Snakes, with their sinuous, secretive movements and sudden appearances bring potent energy into any story realm. A snake that speaks may be able to lead a character where he or she has never gone before. Benevolent and rapid as a wind in the grass, it may help a human being to take hold of distance and time and to enter into places that would otherwise have been sealed away. The snake's ability to penetrate deeply into dark places has brought about its association with the principle of evil. Yet, its power of entry and of swift propulsion can also strengthen a character's forward progress. Fear inspires risk. Risks taken that turn into good bring refreshing new courage and trust in life. The appearance of such a teacher in a story landscape may squeeze life out of those who are unwilling to receive its lessons. A story character's ability to listen to the sibilant hissing of a snake's voice may lead him or her to discern the good snake from the bad, the helping one from the one with intent to harm.

Two snakes intertwined around the Tree of Life are pictured on the Aesculepian staff of healing. They are representatives of the energies that interpenetrate in every human spinal cord. Representatives of these two snakes may be met in a story, their mysterious eyes able to see through gloom and darkness, their darting tongues able to sing, however strangely, about the true cause of an illness of a particular heart, body, mind, or of a body politic. One who is given the grace to hear their singing and to know its meaning can bring great healing wisdom to others in a story realm. The tree on which they twine may also speak great truths for those willing to listen to its rustling speech and to respect what they hear. A journey taken to find this vital tree may take a story character far and wide until the tree is found – perhaps in his or her own garden. What is deep within us sometimes must be seen as outside in order for us to accept it as part of ourselves.

A great and wise snake in a story may also be able to teach a story figure about the human chakra energy system, that is closely connected with the snakelike nerve cord within every backbone. As you accept your natural fear of the snakelike powers within you, you can picture them as offering venom and also wise medicine. You can look deeply into yourself to find the snakelike forms and characteristics that live and move in everyone.

Let a friendly and enlivening snake lead a protagonist where he or she has never been before.

Tell a story about one or two snakes who are physicians in disguise. With their eyes they can see into whatever is opposed to life. The Tree of Life, itself, is their medical office, a place that protects and inspires terrific standards of health and vitality. Bring a part of yourself, which is not as well as it might be, to this splendid office, and let these wise snakes twine through you to diagnose and repair what has gone wrong. Tell this office visit as a story. Who else might you bring to this office?

FLOWERS

Every flower carries healing energies into the world. The qualities of specific plants and flowers can be brought into your stories. Their starlike shapes in leaf and blossom, their exquisite colors, and the aromas that they freely give to all can become story themes. A protagonist who goes in search of a healing herb for an ailing king, bewitched child, or creature in distress may undergo many adventures through fields, gardens, forests, or under water, in order to find just the right one. A quest for a red flower suggests joyous healthy blood, a blue or purple flower spiritual awakening and striving, a yellow flower fresh clear-shining thoughts.

In the fairy tale 'Rapunzel', the mother-to-be craves green rampion, and as a result, she and her husband and child must learn to deal with a witch that guards it. Everyone sometimes has to face the world like a weak king or queen or a lover held in captivity. Flowers, both real and visionary, may come to help and heal your own weak will, heart, and thoughts. You can invite the color, form, fragrance, and vitality of the flowers to fill your story world with their beautiful gifts.

Through a magical story flower, feeling can hold sway and speak. In the Breton classic 'Perronique' the hero enters a garden.

There were roses of all colors, Spanish gorse, red honeysuckle, and above them all rose a fairy flower that was laughing; but a lion with a mane of serpents was running around the garden, rolling his eyes and gnashing his teeth like two freshly ground millstone.

The hero conquers the lion and hurries away with the powerfully laughing flower. When the flower opens, radiant joy bursts out like sunlight, banishing sorrow and fear. The flower helps him to conquer death, to win enduring love, and to overcome the most evil sorcerer in that land. This inner flower is a mysterious aspect of all human beings.

Another potent flower appears in the old German tale 'Jorinda and Joringel'. Joringel first saw it in a dream vision and began to seek it over hill and dale until, early in the morning of the ninth day of his search, he found 'the blood-red flower'. What he had found gave him absolute protection so that he could spring open doors to an enchanted castle. This mysteriously robust red flower opened all the cages in which the witch had held multitudes of young women captive in the disguise of pale birds. It is an emblem of the health that flows from soul to soul when true love perseveres against obstacles.

The first time I decided to cast my own life struggle directly into a fairy tale I was very sad and at my wit's end. My relationship with a friend, who loved gardening, had broken down and I needed somehow to find perspective and consolation. I started writing early one spring morning, and by the middle of the day I had finished and was feeling better. I shared the story with people who would understand it, and through their listening found that I was feeling even better. Eventually I even sent the story to him, though I knew parts of it would be difficult for him to read. My story began:

Once there lived a youthful old king who was vital and noble and strove for the good of all his land. When the green cape of this king fell open, it revealed a splendid breastplate upon which shone a finely etched rosebush with golden and silver leaves; over his eager heart the green and red roots of the rose clasped an emerald and a ruby.

He entered into a very deep forest with his retinue of lords and ladies. There, during the story, he literally lost his head; it was replaced by a frightening troll's head. I was amazed to find myself writing:

Then, in place of the king stood a troll in a king's body. Wrath reigned now in his cold heart – ingratitude and lust. His tones were tyrannical shouts, commands, and reproaches. Overwhelming ugliness was flowing from his eyes and flooding all he saw. His retinue drew away. Was this their playfellow, their king? The birds ceased singing. The bush on his breastplate that had shone so nobly in the morning light, now had shriveled to an ignoble thornbush. The healing jewels of red and green fell out on to the dark and tangled grasses.

Only after writing the story did his complex behavior make sense to me. I wrote:

And from that time forth, new powers of truth grew within him. He knew the dark places. Melody held sway in his soul – now he could sing in tune. Gratitude shone like a rose in his heart. And the owl watched truly over the troll until it grew old and went over the waterfall, with its one terrible head left and its bitter, loveless rages, and died.

Connecting this man with the rose had helped me to see into the thorny depths of his behavior. The language brought me out of myself. I was joyful I had found this hygienic method for dealing with my own pain and bewilderment. Writing the story as it came to me showed me much that I had not been able to accept or to see clearly with my rational mind.

One evening in early summer I asked an art therapeutic group to write a story in which three flowering plants give their gifts to a needy traveler. I spoke about the work of Edward Bach and others who have felt deeply into the plant world. A social worker, who had the habit of giving her time and care to others so completely that she was unable to enjoy any of her free time, wrote about Zeba, a six-year-old orphan, outcast from her mountain village.

She was hungry, tired, and felt very weak. Yet she walked and walked on. People would pass her and not question why this child was alone, dirty, and sickly. Eventually, she fell to the ground. Frightened as she lay there, she felt a quiver beneath her right ear. After a time she realized the quivering was coming from the roots of an old olive tree. She waited, receptive to what the roots might say. And talk they did!! They spoke softly and lovingly calling her name. 'Zeba, you are of us. You are a child of earth. You are full of loving goodness and beauty like us.'

For Zeba in her short lifetime, this experience was unique. She felt as if she belonged, as if she were part of a whole! She went beyond her emptiness and loneliness. She felt refreshed, as if she had partaken of a bounteous feast. Zeba cried, feeling so moved, so loved.

The roots said, 'We will always be here; we are of you and you of us'. They urged her to visit the violets by the roadside two miles beyond. The violets, sending their faces to the heavens, beckoned her to lie down in their arms, as she was of them and they were of her. She felt the healing grace of their spirits filling every cell in her body.

The story of Zeba helped this woman to accept herself very deeply and to go home to a sweet night of rest.

Tell a story in which plants of different colors, odors, and qualities help a weary traveler. To become very sensitive to plants, you might read *Flower Essences and Vibrational Healing* by Gurudas and the biography of Edward Bach who discovered the Bach Flower Remedies.

Envision a flower that is like a magic wand. What qualities does it protect or bring about? Who wields it in your story?

TREES

You, like all human beings, are a walking tree, mysteriously in touch with all human history and with the universe. The Tree of Life and the Tree of Knowledge are twining together within you. The vital trees of your circulatory, nerve, and other vital systems bind you to all trees that are rooted in the earth. The sun, moon and stars, winds and water, all the elements in the earth are feeding you. The Norse 'Edda' pictures the world as one cosmic Tree – Iggdrasil. Heaven, Earth, and Hell are held in its branches, trunk, and roots. The human beings created on middle earth were believed to be tender saplings, little microcosmic children of the Great Tree. All story trees may be representatives of this one Great Tree.

The dark wood in which you sometimes feel you are wandering or caught, though it may be filled with dark and tangled roots and foliage, has within it pathways that lead to enlightenment. Dante came upon 'a dark wood,' which was the antechamber to his own pictures of Inferno. Such Cambrian depths are what we sometimes feel when we picture our mind or body as a destructive organism, holding us in darkness and shadows. We can feel our selves to be a thicket or an endless forest that conceals wicked, fearful forms. Yet caring, gentle, luminous ones may join us in there too. Pathways through these tangled forests of our inner selves – lush, wild, dry, cold, hot, sinister as they may be – will bring us to bright spots. Clearings may be burning or filled up with snow and ice. All the seasons may pass through them again and again in a twinkle, showing us times past and times future. Flowers and sweetest music may well up from their earth, like water from a fountain. A saint may wander into such a clearing, offering wise words and joy. A witch may try to hold us in an enchanted structure of her own design, or a beast may keep beautiful gardens there, longing for Beauty to stay and disenchant him. Such story pictures activate our interweaving connections with all that surrounds us, protecting and stimulating new growth. In the Grimm's tale 'Many-furs', the princess who flees from her father's incestuous love walks the whole night until she reaches a great forest, and then she falls asleep in a hollow tree. Concealed within its protective sheaths of bark, she gathers her strength to go on. The king's son who finds her there thinks she is a wild beast until at last she proves to him, and also to herself, that she, like the tree, carries within her noble, celestial circulations.

A child of five, entertaining her family with a story, told about a very large tree, not quite as tall as the sky.

'It was 2,000 years old', she said very mysteriously. 'It would never, never die.' A cloud came to cover and protect it from a giant who wanted to eat it. But because of the cloud he could not find it. When the giant was nearby some very special stones that lived under this tree pretended they were peas so he would never know what they were and take them away.

She was very pleased with her story.

Tell the story of a tree that overcomes three great obstacles and receives many gifts on its upward journey to the sun. Let this tree represent you or someone you know and love.

Let a story figure in great distress find safety inside a hollow tree deep in a sacred wood. Let the tree sing to your wanderer, cradling her safely until she is ready to be delivered, like a baby, into new hands.

7

Power and Protection

Storytelling is to change the world.
— Brother Blue, Master of Storytelling

SHOES AND CROWNS

Storytelling helps us to picture the healthy potentates within us who take life in stride. Standing at a refreshing distance with them, we can look out over familiar vistas and enter new territories. In your stories, shoes may take on a life of their own. They can lead one of your wanderers on to new pathways or homeward safely with unprecedented ease. With new boots or shoes a character, like Puss-in-Boots, suddenly may be able to leap over mountains and cover vast distances in a short space of time. Whoever makes shoes of such special qualities must be a special shoemaker, whose needle and diligence and excellent skill allow these powers to flow through the leather and threads. Perhaps threads of moonlight and starlight will inhere in the soles and insteps of heavenly dancing slippers. Snake-skin boots might be oiled with venom that casts dark shadows wherever a culprit goes. Moccasins sewn from buck sinew strengthen the footsteps of an eager brave. Spirited shoes may also turn into shoes of justice, such as the burning shoes the evil stepmother must wear at the end of the original version of the story of Cinderella. A fiery dance of death also ends 'Rumplestiltskin'. In 'The Juniper Tree' the bright red shoes that the bird boy drops as a gift for his sister signify the joyous love they have for one another, which no evil can destroy. Sometimes shoes must be cast off or buried in order to free feet for another kind of movement.

In other stories crowns take on special significance. A crown is a shining connection with ultimate power and glory. One who receives a golden crown may be lifted into ineffable wholeness. Crowns signify great responsibility and deep commitment to others. A crowning signifies hope of wise, radiant leadership. A poor shepherd or hunchback or a fool becomes a prince in countless stories. Within everyone is the hope that, as we progress through our many trials, we ultimately are destined for a royal seat. In our sometimes awkward and uncouth goodness and strength, we feel the seeds of greatness – and so we recognize true royal qualities, or the lack thereof, in the leaders we follow.

Just as shoes and feet may carry us on a journey to a throne, so the lowest mortal may strive toward, and sometimes in life and in stories, attain great happiness, self-mastery, power, and love. Story wisdom safeguards the attainment of the crown for the gentle, pure souls who in the end often receive the kingdom. Yet crowns at the start of a story are sometimes in the possession of tyrants whose power must be usurped by higher moral forces. If an old king sets seemingly vicious tasks for the simple one to perform, story wisdom teaches us that these tasks can be accomplished, even to the amazement of all. In the story 'Perronique', the hero overcomes personifications of death, greed, and evil to win his crown and also his true love.

The secret crown which you carry always as a human being uplifts and ennobles you, connecting you with the spiritual working of the universe. Magical shoes in your stories can connect you with the whole earth and whatever expanses your story figures explore beyond the confines of earthly gravity.

Imagine a crown. See its qualities clearly. Is it made of gold, of silver, of moonbeams? Is it modest, demure, grandiose, splendid, harmonious? Is it of solid matter or of ethereal substance? Perhaps it is made of mosses and seeds or of crystals of different kinds and potencies. If it is a flower crown, see its colors and shapes as alive and fragrant with many healing qualities. Is it a nestful of singing birds or made of spiderwebs? Or shaped like a Balinese temple, full of little swinging golden and crystal bells. Who is wearing this crown? The one who is wearing the crown becomes the central figure in your story. Give him or her a name, a realm, and a purpose. A decree goes out. When the decree is made, then others must come to bring it to full realization.

Create an imaginary shoemaker whose work it is to supply the exact shoes needed by whomever knocks at his or her door. Imagine a cripple who receives shoes that allow full movement and a wicked one whose shoes stop it in its tracks and weld it to the earth.

GOWNS AND MANTLES

Putting clothing on and taking it off is a humdrum daily activity.

Yet through the resonance of your imagination such a simple action can shimmer with powerful and mysterious meaning. The receiving of a beautiful dress by a princess or a young queen is a great event in many old tales. Cinderella's three dancing gowns, in the original story, are given by an angelic bird that lives in the tree above her mother's grave. The gowns descend upon the girl as gifts from the purely spiritual life to which her mother returned at her death. Each gown the daughter receives has distinct qualities: one as radiant as the moon, one as shining as the sun, and one reflects radiance from all the stars. When the maiden is ready to seek the partner of her soul, her true prince, then she can experience the celestial confluences – symbolized in the holy dresses – which guide her into loving partnership with him.

A similar set of gowns is given to many young, striving souls as they ascend the staircase to their own full identities as partners in the great royal dance of life and love that ends so many old stories. Sometimes these gowns were carried in 'nutshells' or in sacks until they were ready to come forth. Allerleirauh disguised herself in furs before she fled from her libidinous father's castle carrying her gowns securely in a nut until she could find a wiser realm in which to realize love.

When a hero receives a cloak, it may give him the power of invisibility or of protection in conflict or battle. With a magical cloak he may be able to travel swiftly, even fly, to a destined goal. Or when it is on his shoulders, he may be able to wish for whatever his heart desires. Gowns shimmer in the air around the budding princess or the queen in full flower, like a celestial nimbus; cloaks tend to be grounded and straight. Together they make up a whole, both necessary in a well-rounded story, in which male and female characters are taken as parts of everyone by unbiased listeners.

In story language, you can see and accept the radiant garments of your soul's complete identity. You can put on and take off gowns of your celestial nature and mantles of strength and courage and manly perseverance.

A woman, who cared deeply for a man she had divorced, wrote a seventeen-page story for him on his thirty-fifth birthday. Her former husband's mother had killed herself when he was a boy. For years he had been struggling to recover from the shock and confusion of this event and to find his true self. Her story cast him as a glass prince, son of a glass mother. It gave her joy to have recreated his life through positive imagination. As the story began:

A king cursed his wife with a cruel spell – he changed her into a woman of glass. Their unborn child was made of glass too and could easily shatter. To seek help, the young queen left the castle in the dead of night and entered an enchanted wood, where she was taken in by a witch in disguise. At last the babe was born. At the sight of the helpless glass prince, the queen's sorrow increased. 'You must help my son', she said to the witch. 'Isn't there a thing you can do for him?'

'There is one thing', replied the witch. 'I can give him impenetrable armor, which will prevent him from breaking.' 'Then you must do it immediately', said the queen.

The witch took a small black pouch from her pantry. She then sprinkled a shadowy substance from it over the body of the tiny glass prince. Instantly his appearance changed. At the same moment he began to cry.

'My, you've broken the spell', cried the queen. 'He's no longer made of glass.'

'Wrong', said the witch. 'That is the armor you see. Very fleshlike, isn't it? No one will be able to tell that he is a glass prince.'

'But why is he crying?', asked the queen, as she bent to stroke his face. 'Ah', she cried, 'this armor burns like fire. Take it off, witch. It is hurting him.'

'It can only be removed if he himself speaks the word "armor"', said the witch.

'But he can't speak. Witch, how wicked and cruel you are. Oh, what shall I do?' In her agony the queen stumbled over a marble chair, fell to the stone floor, and broke into countless pieces.

As this story went on,

The prince grew and because of his enchanted armor burned many in his search for love. At last he met a princess who understood his dilemma. The princess said, 'There is something that prevents you from being touched by anyone or anything'.

'That's not true', cried the prince.

'Your mother meant it for your protection', the princess continued, 'but if you don't give it up, you will never be free.'

'I don't know what you are talking about', said the prince.

'It is that which burned us – that which ever burns you', she said.

His eyes went wide. 'My armor?', he cried. As he spoke the word, the armor vanished, and for the first time since he was a baby, the prince was transparent and vulnerable. He startled the princess with a cry of pure ecstasy. 'The burning is gone!'

'Be careful', said the princess, 'you could break now.'

'I don't care', he shouted and dove into the deep spring pool. Now he could be touched with love too.

After the author of this story had shared it with her former husband, she wrote: 'To show you how real the armor in the story is – after he read the story he asked me, "Was this supposed to have something to do with me?" However it may have affected his life, the images and plot rang true for her. Creating her story had been a greatly liberating experience. She had imagined her husband freed from his painfully protective shell.

Another woman wanted to help her colleague and friend overcome an inherited skin disease which she felt was part of his defense against a cruel world. In her tongue-in-cheek story, she pictured his total defense system as a splendid suit of armor,

... an impeccable fortress against any arrow or sword. The growing boy, wondering how the world would appear from behind the tiny eye slits of his helmet, discovered it was a much narrower and inhibited viewpoint. Leopold could see only that which was directly in front of him and at eye-level height. Inside the armor he imagined himself to look gallant and noble. He was transformed into a mighty warrior thirsting for battle. He was proud of his manhood and ready for life! Yet when at last he had grown large enough to put on the full suit, he could not get it off again. When he tried to raise the visor of the helmet, it would not budge. With the helmet stuck in place, Leopold could not see to find the many snaps and hooks and straps that joined the armor plates together. In fact, he was trapped – imprisoned in his *splendid suit of armor.*

Leopold proudly suffered many encounters until at last a little boy found him. The little boy had a beautiful, kind sister and a wise mother. The stiff formalities of manhood, oiled and tapped by this benevolent trio, fell away. Then the little boy and the brave knight walked hand in hand down the hill to the cottage where the smells of dinner rose to greet them.

The author of this beautiful story was also disappointed when she found what she felt was the right moment to share it with her colleague. She wanted to show him what he did not understand about himself, but he had very little interest in her story. Yet in the process of writing it, she had enlightened herself considerably about the path his eventual healing might take.

Another woman created an unusually tactile story:

As the girl touched the snake, it immediately shed its skin and was transformed into seven pieces of cloth that the girl could wear to carry her off beyond the forest. The first dress she put on was a patchy hardened cloth. It allowed no thorns to penetrate her – it protected her from all the tangles she encountered getting to the edge of the forest. The next dress became slightly lighter and more flowing as she was now free of the thorns. When she came to the last dress, this one was like skin, soft, smooth, and flowing.

As she put it on, she had arrived at the edge of the great glistening sea: it enabled her to jump right into the water and swim with all her might.

At the end of this story the girl became a princess and had long flowing dresses to wear always.

Create a story in which a garment serves as protection for its wearer during certain adventures. Then, allow him or her to cast it off or to put it away with appropriate gratitude and perhaps, also, with relief. Allow a hero or heroine to receive a garment that connects him or her with the stars of his or her birth and helps guide and move them toward their destiny. Let the story portray the occasion(s) for which these garments are worn.

GOLDEN BALL

A number of old tales show us a child who is playing with a ball or hoop of gold that is inadvertently lost. It may disappear down a well, as in 'The Frog Prince'; or into the cage of a wildman who has been found, perhaps, in a wild lake in a dark woods as in 'Iron Hans'. Or, it may be lost behind the church as in 'Childe Roland'. The child's playful attachment to this shining, rolling ball, made of the holiest of metals, leads him or her on to great new adventures. These befall until it is as if the ball has returned when the resolution comes, and a larger more complete sense of wholeness has been attained. What had been a child's plaything rolled exactly to where the teachers and life-lessons were waiting. Every child undergoes such crucial transitions, when a sense of safety is lost to a larger world. The ball symbolizes the ever-larger ripples of our circumference as we find our way into and out of whatever experiences we may need in order to grow. It is also symbolic of that golden center-point in which we are all held as we go forth to seek our larger self. The wisdom that is shining within us helps us to sense and to go on seeking the finest qualities of life and love. The child within you plays with the sense of wholeness. When it seems to be lost, you can feel assured that a lesson is in store for you as you seek to find it again.

A mother of three young children, who needed control, was terrified at first to tell a story that wasn't directly from a book. One day, however, she returned home to find that an irresponsible babysitter had let her children wreak havoc inside and outside their house. She wanted to scream.

> I told the babysitter to go. Everything was unhinged. I was at my wit's end. But I set a fire in the fireplace and sat down in the rocking chair. Suddenly I spotted my son's red ball at my feet as I rocked. I didn't know what to do to bring us all together. It was the strangest experience. The story just came out of me. In my story a boy bounced a red ball. It bounced and bounced until it bounced up into the clouds. From there it bounced all the way to the sun and to the moon. Then it bounced down again; it had turned into a golden ball. I couldn't believe such a simple story could make everything all right. I was stunned. It was only a five-minute story! Since then storytelling has become a dramatic and

significant part of our lives. It is as if the stories are out there all the time, waiting for me to recognize them.

Imagine a story in which the main character(s) enter a sphere, like an iridescent bubble that can float anywhere. A great wind carries this luminous, translucent ball to where many new perspectives can be seen.

Imagine seven different-colored balls, layered inside each other like the rings of an onion. Let each layer represent a story episode in a journey toward the golden center, which may represent a potent seed, a healing stone, an essence of joy.

Envision a sacred shining sphere that rolls away from your childhood self to be found in a place where you had to learn important lessons. Tell your personal story as if you are in a fairy tale of your own creation.

TOUCHSTONES AND TALISMANS

Any small gift of transformation and healing that a protector passes into the hands of your story characters can further universal progress. It can connect its bearer with higher powers that have been sent to them for their own advancement. Confusion and helplessness beset everyone. Sometimes a sorry state persists for a long time until, in stories, as in life, a redeemer appears wearing invisibility, or perhaps angel's wings or a ragged jacket or jester's cap. From this mysterious one a gift is offered. It fits in the pocket or slips quickly on to a finger or around a wrist, bearing the vibrations of pure goodness, of the ordering power of the universe and the kindness of love. The exact nature of the stone may be of interest to you as a storyteller. A birthstone, rhodochrosite, lepidolite, bloodstone, dark or clear crystal – all carry distinct qualities, as flowers do, for healing. The stone may be nondescript except that it is charged with the loving powers of its giver. From that moment the touchstone gives faith and ardor to the one who has received it.

Talismans also appear in stories – curious objects carved with insignia and other symbolic signs. When a talisman has been found on a path or given, like a touchstone, it confers certain supernatural gifts. It may have been given by a wise potentate in a great public ceremony, or may have come in a quiet, unexpected moment from a guardian spirit or a kindly witch, or have been dropped by an angelic sparrow on the wing specifically to transform a situation.

Perhaps it has been found while the protagonist is digging potatoes or pouring water from a jug.

I asked a group of nine- to eleven-year-olds to make up a story in groups of two or three about kindness triumphing over its opposite. Two of them made up a story drama, using puppets and colored cloths to represent the castle, the lake, and the forest where dark and light were weaving around a wise woman.

The princess requested permission from her mother, the queen, to play by the lake with the beautiful view.

'Very well, my daughter, enjoy yourself.'

The princess took her beloved crystal with her. When it had disappeared, she did not notice at first. Then she wept intensely. 'Duck', she pleaded, 'have you seen anything fall in the lake? Could you search for me?' The queen mother awaited her daughter in her throne room. 'My daughter, wouldn't you like another crystal?'

'No. No. No.' The princess wept continuously in her room for many days. When she emerged, she felt different. Selfish. 'Silly to weep over such a little thing. Yes, buy me another one!'

'Something is terribly wrong with the girl', said the queen mother. Nevertheless, a force was compelling the princess to search for her crystal, though she no longer cared for it. The queen went out into the forest where dark and light weave. She went to find the wise American Indian woman, Feathers of Truth.

'O kind Feathers of Truth, my daughter has had a beloved crystal with her since the day she was born. She has loved it so much, her kindness bore into it. When the crystal was swept into the waves of our lake, all her kindness and unselfishness were swept into the waves with it. What shall I do about my unkind, selfish, and impolite daughter? O shamaness, after her return she took on these characteristics.'

'The stone must be retrieved by your daughter. No one can do it for her', were the wise one's words.

'Search', said the queen. 'Your crystal was a gift from your father

and me. I am commanding you.'

The princess searched. 'O it is probably lost in the mud.' She slept, and when she awoke, she felt different. 'I must search at the lake', she said. Once more she approached the duck for help.

'Swim to that gold patch there out on the water.' (The narrator put a small golden cloth over a blue one and had the duck puppet swim to it.)

The duck dove through the gold and blue until it disappeared under them and found the crystal.

'O thank you. How can I ever thank you? It isn't muddy at all.' The princess returned to inform her mother of her good fortune. 'I found it!' 'We shall have a great celebration', sang the good queen. Then they shared a long and joyous embrace.

Tell a story in which a magic talisman is given, lost, and found again. Let this talisman represent an aspect of your own heart.

Picture a stone that gives you pleasure. Perhaps it has fallen out of a piece of heirloom jewelry or is your 'birthstone'. To learn about the vibrational and moral qualities of common and uncommon stones, consult one of the many books now available. Take an innocent protagonist on a journey in which this stone reveals its significance.

SEEDS AND NUTS

Whether you tell a tale that is light-hearted or serious, a magical seed or nut in the possession of one of your characters may indicate fabulous surprises are in store. A huge, beneficent oak is contained in the little nugget of an acorn. With their exact divisions between the two lobes, walnuts especially resemble human brains. When something important is kept in a nut and stays secretly folded away, it is as if what had been full-blown has been reabsorbed into a concentrated seed. It may have folded up neatly within it a magical table, which whenever it is needed can always provide food and drink for a weary traveler. This nurturing nut fits neatly into his pocket. A spell may need to be spoken for its goodness to be released – a mantra that unites its material substance with its essence. Perhaps it has been in the possession of a gnome or a wise woman who has given it to someone, perhaps as a token of gratitude. It demonstrates the strength and beauty that can flow from even the tiniest mustard seed of a good deed. In some stories the whole universe is contained within the enchanted nut, carried by a princess until she is prepared to unfold the fullness of her own cosmic robes by giving herself truly to love.

Your walnut-brain is a mysterious seed of the whole universe.

Milk and honey, a generous table of plenty, encircling gowns of starry beauty, mantles and wands of wisdom and might, are hidden in the mysterious nut-like folds of your mind that you can let unfold in your stories.

Picture a seed – its color and shape and size. Let your story seed fall into earth that is either unfriendly or welcoming. Rejecting earth or sweet fertile earth has its immediate effects on the little seed. Let the seed sleep, and, then, let it awaken. Its roots search for the nutrients it needs. Perhaps, if it is obstructed by rock or asphalt, it may receive a great boon of sunlight or a crystal song from a nearby stream. As it reaches up to the light, let it feel its joyous expansion from smallness to greatness.

Tell a story about a nut that contains a precious power, which you have not been able to express fully, if at all, in your life. During your story let a wise one speak the words that release the nut's hidden power. After this nut unfolds, perhaps there might be a celebration in your story at which a king, a queen, and all their royal realm are present.

GOLDEN BOWL

Deep in the heart of every human being shines an invisible bowl. Into it are received all the gifts that are given to us from others: their words, gestures, and loving thoughts. The search for a golden bowl is an ancient and sacred one. An old mother, a beggar's child, a surfacing turtle may be the wise one to bestow this bowl. It may be found in a hollow tree or a castle keep, and although worn or cracked, it may be felt to represent the inner heart of receptivity. One who wanders without a bowl may be unable to receive the offerings of others and fall ill as a result. Perhaps the capacity for receptivity has been lost or has been thrown carelessly aside and turned into a rough cracked bowl. Yet having been lost a bowl can be found again. A tarnished, cracked bowl may secretly be a golden one, like a prince in disguise.

In the mysteries of the Holy Grail when the power to receive goodness and plenty has been returned to the king, he is cured of illness and his radiant health shines out to all his kingdom and the landscape. The Grail-king's castle is like the castle in 'Princess Thornrose' that is brought back to life by the power of love. The dry despair of the aged Grail-king and the deep withdrawal from life of the adolescent princess are both aspects of ourselves. These, when we are experiencing true love, dissolve into joyous vitality.

In my round basket full of hand puppets, kings and queens, paupers and serving-maids, princesses and dummlings, snakes and bears sleep jumbled with exotic witches and shamans. Over the basket I wrap cloths of vibrant colors and there the puppets rest, archetypes under cover. One Saturday afternoon, as I was giving a course for adults in my home, I asked everyone to choose two puppets and to allow them, one on either hand, to relate to one another. An American Indian brave and a wicked-looking wizard found their way on to the hands of a 'workaholic'. A struggle ensued. The brave danced free from the red cloth and exulted above the man's head, meanwhile the left-hand puppet objected strenuously and tried to get the brave down again by sitting on him. At the other side of the circle a young African princess on a woman's right hand unwound slowly from a ghostly silk and was wound up again and again by the imposing veiled presence on her other hand.

I asked these two to embark with their puppets on a journey to a place of beauty and to deal with any obstacles they found along the way. As they had already warmed to the occasion through this previous exercise, they had no difficulty beginning at once to dialogue with one another.

The brave announced that he very much wanted to seek a chalice he had heard of that contained an elixir which would allow him to feel whole. 'You are whole. You look whole', said his story companion.

'Yes, but I don't feel whole.'

So they set out together. Almost immediately they came to a Slough of Despondency, which they built up out of dark-colored cloths at their knees as they continued to speak. Together they found a way to enlist the service of the keeper of that slough. Having left the keeper behind, the two traveled on (moving across my living room floor to the edge of my couch). 'Ah, a Sea of Danger, of anger!' (I put a long red cloth out and they knelt, puppets in hand, to deal with this new challenge. They dialogued for a time, their voices almost inaudible with the depth of their feeling.) The puppet-figure in the sea gradually wrapped them into the depths of its red power until they were totally enveloped in it. After a time they discovered that, nevertheless, they were not of it and climbed out.

Then they came to a Land of Purity. Now they were much closer to their goal and the brave said that he could almost taste the elixir. The sun was glowing outside the window beyond the puppets. In their excitement they talked reverently and with unprecedented honesty about the ice cream and other tastes that had kept them from this goal.

'This is scary', said the brave.

'It is for me too', said his companion.

'We can do this without ice cream.'

'I want to do the ice cream again.'

'I understand about the ice cream. It is the way you fill the empty place.' They agreed about this.

'I am willing to take a chance if you are.'

'If we put our hearts together, mine will be broken when you take yours away.'

'No. I will lose myself if we put ourselves together.' 'Isn't it possible to be separate and one at the same time?'

The puppet adventurers came to a windowpane and stared out at a luminous vision. The chalice beckoned. How to get through the glass together? 'Let us put our minds together and create a thought that will take us through.'

'I think we will have to join more than our minds, our hearts, perhaps even our bodies.' They wrapped the puppets together. They leaned into the light and drank.

Let a symbolic bowl become badly cracked or broken into many pieces in the course of your story. By what mending process does your bowl become whole again?

One by one let your story characters go in search, unsuccessfully, of the bowl or chalice that will restore warm, wholesome feeling to a cold, unfeeling land. At the end of your story, let the bowl be found by a child who can see into secret places. Who guards and guides this child? How is this bowl received by others after it has been found?

LANCE, SWORD, AND WAND

Since storytelling began, weapons have flashed and lurked creating excitement, astonishment and grief, and obsession with a means of protection and retaliation. Stories that demonstrate the intelligent use of power bring peace and ease into the hearts of young and old alike.

From the old mystery schools of Chartres and other centers of wise instruction emanated the tale of a great angel-hero who could lead people to the truth. His power was seen as a sword that, whether coming from his mouth or hand, radiated golden shining light. This sword is concentrated energy, focusing great physical power and penetrating insights. It is like an eye or a cosmic arm of the inner self that allows its bearer to perceive and to wield power even to the stars. This eye and arm can see and reach into the good and evil designs of the universe.

The story of 'Saint George and the Dragon' has come through many centuries with a thousand-and-one subtle variations. Saint George, in the old English story, is an emblem of this noble truth-wielding figure. Sometimes he has been shown sending his sword down the chaotic throat of a dragon, sometimes penetrating into its dark heart. When he has subdued the dragon, new life springs forth full of love, celebrations, and fresh ennobling resolve.

A rounded sword does not kill. It represents willingness to meet the enemy without loss of life, limb, or property. Its killing point is carried within, to transform the destructive impulse in oneself and in others. This 'sword' of true compassion, wielded by Mahatma Gandhi and countless others throughout history, is worn by those who have the ability to stand truly upright in their stories, having conquered the need to hide behind weapons and other devices of secrecy and aggression. Their whole body has been penetrated with this sword of light.

In the mythology of the search for the Holy Grail, the grail knight seeks to find and to comprehend a lance that will return health to the king and to all his land. The mythical lance of life may be seen, like a magical wand, to be living within all human beings. The lance is a portion of the Tree of Life that, though it be torn away, may spring again into the possession of its owner. Sometimes the lance is used as a weapon against an evil force. It may also be pictured as a walking stick, with buds and fruits whirled into its wood. Whenever it is shattered or lost, sorrow, weakness, and deprivation follow. To all who hold and wield it well, honest peace and plenitude come.

In the traditional lore of certain American Indian tribes, wands of power are constructed according to the rites of the community, with sacred stones and herbs entwined with plant or animal bindings. These may become rods of power capable of bringing about many kinds of changes. As a storyteller, you have the power to bestow these instruments into the hands of your characters, for weal or for woe. In your story realms you can find and take up sword, lance, and wand – potent with wisdom – so that the good may prevail.

A girl of ten made up a story about a queen who possessed a magical sceptre. Looking into its point, said the young storyteller, the queen could see 'all of the bad things that were happening in her kingdom and how she could correct them'. When this staff was lost, a 'harsh layer of anger and bitterness took over her life'. However, at the end of the story, the magical staff-of-life was returned with great jubilation and the queen's visionary powers flourished again.

In the landscape and progress of a story, describe the deeds that must be done to transform fear into love.

Tell the story of a wandering wand-maker who goes through centuries and lands creating an endless variety of these sparkling instruments of transformation.

8

How to Nurture Storytelling

*Tell the story for all time, so that every
grain of sand and every worm that ever
will be hears it. – Brother Blue,
Master of Storytelling*

Speech is often used less to express
genuine feelings and thoughts than to
hide, veil or deny them. – Alice Miller

Because there is a natural storytelling urge and ability in all human beings, even just a little nurturing of this impulse can bring about astonishing and delightful results. Children who are encouraged by listening to the stories told by their elders will often create exquisite and profound ones, even at a very early age. Parents who did not experience storytelling in their own families as they were growing up can discover wonderful abilities, which have been waiting perhaps for many years to come forth, hidden within them. Children, especially during their waking and going-to-sleep times, can inspire our best stories. The springs of imagination well up freely through them. Sitting close to children and looking deeply into their eyes, one can often find just the right beginnings and energies for the stories they need to hear.

A scientist has told or read a story to his son almost every night for nine years. His son is now twelve, very sensitive yet full of confidence in many activities. The father spoke about the importance of storytelling in their family. 'As long as I keep going a story unfolds', he said.

It is quite a remarkable thing to watch it happening before my very eyes. I find there is always something in my stories about myself, a memory thread, perhaps with a little twist. Usually I also throw in a little magic, and I try to put in humor. My stories are not necessarily wild flights of imagination. When our son was young, I just told stories about real things and what had happened to him during the day but cast in story form. I changed his name to Joey. Strange how events that happened to him would happen to Joey in a similar way! No great messages. Getting up. Activities with our family. Meals. Just reaffirming his own experiences.

Every evening we were making a connection with one another. He was with me. I learned that in his eyes my stories were never failures. In this way I discovered what a bond could grow between a parent and a child. One of my greatest objections to TV is that it robs parents of this kind of creative time with their children. We want our son to trust his own imaginative powers, his ability to make judgments and to act. So far, the stories are my way of getting that over to him.

The imaginative happening for the child becomes a powerful tool later on in life. I see this in my own work. People should not belittle the power of imagination and intuition to guide activities. The world would grind to a halt if we had to wait for science to give us all the answers about how to live.

The wife of this remarkable man has always shown deep and lively interest in his stories, yet does not interfere with the relationship that is possible between father and son because of the storytelling they share, a time of rest and refreshment away from technological input. Sometimes the parents collaborate with their son to weave some aspect of the story through their day.

Whether telling stories with your children or strangers, one of the most useful guiding principles is to style their language and imagery to the prevailing mood of whomever may be listening. A fiery person will not be impressed with a languid plot. Similarly, an excitable group that lives on high energy will not be easily calmed down until some elements of their own mood have caught their attention: a fire-breathing monster, a wild storm, a commanding, demanding potentate. Whoever loves light, laughter, and playful antics will not be drawn to profoundly tragic episodes. A contented listener will probably prefer a slow-moving, well-ordered story. A sad listener will probably prefer to have at least one character who is struggling with burdensome realities.

As a storyteller you can turn even very ordinary events, people, and things into many-layered, many-faceted symbolic pictures. A group of parents, who wanted to create a school for their children out of their own ideals, met to explore storytelling. One evening we worked with the story of 'Briar Rose' for several hours. First we read the story aloud slowly, passing the book from hand to hand around the circle. After some explorations of the image of the thorn-rose wall that protected the princess in her deep sleep, I asked them to write. I said, 'Imagine that you yourself are a thorn wall. Go into the thornbush of teenage defences.

Begin with an 'I am' statement, such as 'I am a thorny rose'.

One unusually practical mother surprised herself greatly when she wrote:

> *I am an imposing thorny patch.*
> *I cannot get through to anyone,*
> *nor can anyone get through to me.*
> *It's hard to give love without a sting.*
> *It's hard to accept love without a smart.*
> *How can I get to the loving beauty that I know exists?*
> *What can change the riveting pincushion I've become?*
> *Insensitive to others. Insensitive to myself.*
> *When will I awaken and feel the welcome softness?*

Everyone read aloud, and drew with crayons for a while. Then I said, 'Write a piece that begins "I am a rose"'. At the end of this piece, the same mother found herself writing: 'My petals and essence, in the golden cask, last till the end of time.' Something had burst wide open within her. She had found herself in a new way.

Several years later she and I remembered this story session. The school had been successfully founded and named after a species of wild rose found in their area. The founding mother said that she had been deeply stirred by the image of the rose wall that was protecting such vulnerable youthful beauty in the story'. Suddenly the book of living imagery had seemed to waken within her. She found that she was able to see and to make connections where before she herself had been asleep. As a homoeopathic practitioner, this reflected deeply in her ability to commune with her patients and their many problems. I had encouraged her to paint and draw to illustrate the stories she told to help the children and their parents experience graphically the remedies she gave them. It gave her pleasure to be creative in this way for the sake of her patients. She did not feel herself to be particularly artistic. Actually, like so many who do not know it, she was astoundingly gifted. As these gifts unfolded, she became more and more confident of her ability to understand and to express the language of symbols. Later she said to me:

When we were naming our school, I could speak very clearly and confidently about what the rose could mean to us. Through storytelling imagery, now, it is as if I can step outside everything then step back in again. I feel that long long ago I was involved with symbols. The great truths behind these are everlasting. I am rediscovering their living significance.

Symbols awaken when you feel them as a living part of yourself. They are discovered through a portal of the mind that takes you deep into formative processes. Your body naturally wants to express health; your soul also seeks to express itself in a healthy way. Healing forces are constantly working to restore balance. Whenever you activate your personal connection with great story images, life-forces are generated from deep within you.

'I am a parched land.'
'I am Hansel in the witch's cage.'
'I am a wheel spinning straw into gold.'
'I am Cinderella at the dark hearth.'
'I am a donkey that wants to make heavenly music.'

Marvelous seeds and springs lie beneath the 'parched land'. The moment you identify with Hansel, you know your sister will be able to liberate you. You feel within you the wheel that whirrs in an emergency and creates a miracle. Your own pure soul, like Cinderella's, bends in the ashes. The donkey within you will not give up until it succeeds in expressing the beauty it feels.

The imaginative world, so full of movement and transformation, is profoundly real. In some ways it resembles children who are playing. Gradually you can orient yourself and interpret what is happening there. You can delight in the discovery of new boundaries around the powerful configurations that move forward and disappear again into the dream depths of your imagination and interweave them with your ordinary consciousness.

Making a regular time with your family to explore these powers of story imagination can put your storytelling on a firm footing. It also helps to join with others outside your family who have the same or similar needs and intentions to explore great story-lore. Once you have read a story aloud within a story group, its grand design will already be working on you.

Almost all great old fairy tales can be told within a relatively short span of time. This is reassuring when you want to make up stories of your own. A story, which fills 15 minutes with well chosen words and a truly satisfactory composition of characters and events, can give joy for a whole lifetime. The test that a story image is truly working is that your heart will feel light and a flame of joy will shine up within it. It may spring to mind and give special significance and momentum to what might otherwise have been unsatisfying or even meaningless moments.

Learning to tell at least one great old story verbatim, with one's whole heart alert to its inner meaning, gives courage for the telling of future tales, whether old ones or new ones that you will invent to meet a special occasion.

Since stories are made up of a series of pictures and sometimes these pictures are very great ones and exist on several levels at once, rather than analyzing, it is often most helpful to use colored crayons, paints, or pencils to illustrate an image or scene in the story that is puzzling or fascinating in some other way. Artistic expertise is not necessary for such efforts to be beneficial. Stories awaken a sense of movement and color and design that helps the conscious mind to contact the essence of a scene or character. Attempts to draw or to paint the layers of meaning from one moment in a story can awaken ability and inspiration for other modes of creativity. A spontaneous song or poem may well forth or a little psycho-drama. A group can return the following week, or at some other regularly scheduled time, to share the results of such inner explorations.

Your imagination loves to be given specific tasks. It thrives when it can go to work to bring about changes through a flow of images.

Some themes that you can take up with others or on your own are listed here:

STORY TRANSFORMATIONS

From	passivity	*to*	hope
	sloth		diligence
	loneliness		oneness
	stubbornness		kindness
	impatience		forbearance
	illness		health
	handicap		gift
	poverty		wealth/contentment
	awkwardness		grace
	rage		love
	vanity/pride		understanding
	hyperactivity		calm
	powerlessness		potency
	confusion		clarity
	addiction		compassion
	lying		courage for the truth
	violence		gentleness
	obsession		openness
	bitterness		tastefulness
	emptiness		fullness
	fear		courage
	stone		music
	monster/automoton		human being
	weaponry		visionary eye
	superficiality		depth
	death		new life

Stimulated by a transformative goal, whether you are alone or with a storytelling group, you may invoke one or more of the aspects of the story worlds that have been set out in this book. When you are exploring a 'bog' mood, for example, you might wish to express this mood more thoroughly – to find ways out of it through the use of imagination that stays true to your situation. Similarly, the sense of gratitude might be explored through story images or wishing. As a group leader, you might present the theme in story terms and guide the offerings of the others in the group. As a group, you can help one another accept the beautiful and powerful images that live within you.

When you experience yourself, even for a moment, as a creator, you touch the creativity through which all things come into being, are sustained, and pass on into other dimensions. Stories that are satisfying express healthy circulation; they breathe delightfully and deeply. A plot that is based on your pulse beat – a regular flow of fours – unfolds in a regular pattern. The central character or characters set out on a journey. First one obstacle is overcome, then a second, and finally a third, releasing the central figures to a radiant sense of unity with the source of well-being. Upon this basic format there are an infinite number of variations. By taking an open, experimental approach to story composition as you work with various themes, characters, landscapes, and moods, this hearty blueprint, which has served aeons of storytellers and story creators, also will serve you.

If you double the basic four-beat then seven tests or obstacles, and perhaps seven rewards, will come to your hero or heroine. In this grand design, your characters may move through the seven tones of a major or minor scale, through the colors of the rainbow spectrum, through the days of the week, or even through the seven 'chakras' of our human bodies until they reach a sense of unity and peace. Another time-honored story sequence is based on three sets of four. Stories based upon the power of twelve can take your protagonists on a journey through the zodiac. In the days leading to a birthday celebration, for example, representatives of all the other signs of the zodiac can be met with the birth-chart symbolic animal acting as guard and guide. Or, the twelve months might be encountered as story figures, each offering its strength and wisdom.

Uniting story imagination with the power of one, two, three, resolving in four, a story ground becomes firmly formed out of the complex numerical wisdom that courses continuously through everyone. Every effort you make to circulate these pulsing heart rhythms in your stories affirms fundamental laws of your nature, which, though they may baffle your mind, nevertheless form the foundation of all lives. Whatever your purpose for making a story, if you summon patterns that have been stored within you and work with these carefully, your story will contain transformative energies. Your sense of who you are and how you meet others and the world, which is evolving, for better or for worse through every sort of human creativity, will hearten and deepen.

Story Bibliography

Other versions of the compendiums and stories mentioned in this book are easily available in local libraries and bookstores, and via the internet. Especially recommended are:

'Allerleirauh', in *The Complete Grimm's Fairytales* (hereafter *CGFT*). New York: Pantheon Books, 1972.

'The Ant and the Grasshopper', in *Aesop's Fables*. Michael Hague, ed. New York: Holt, Rinehart & Winston, 1985.

'Beauty and the Beast', in *Fairy Tales*. Charles Perrault. San Diego: Harcourt Brace Jovanovich, 1986.

'Briar Rose' ('Little Briar Rose', 'Sleeping Beauty'), in *CGFT*.

'Childe Roland', in *English Fairy Tales*, Joseph Jacobs. New York: Dover, 1967.

Chronicles of Narnia, C. S. Lewis. New York: Macmillan, 1983.

'Cinderella', in *CGFT*.

Dear Mili: An Old Tale, Wilhelm Grimm. New York: Farrar, Straus & Giroux, 1988.

'The Devil and the Three Golden Hairs', in *CGFT*.

The Divine Comedy by Dante Alighieri. Geoffrey Bickersteth, ed. London: Basil Blackwell, 1985.

'The Emperor's New Clothes', in *Hans Andersen: 42 Tales*, M. R. James (trans.). New York: A. S. Barnes, 1959.

'Faithful Ferdinand', in *CGFT*.

'The Firebird', in *Russian Fairy Tales*. Aleksandr Afanasev. New York: Pantheon, 1976.

'Fitcher's Bird', in *CGFT*.

'The Fox and the Cat', in *CGFT*.

'The Girl with No Hands' in *CGFT*.

'The Golden Key', in *CGFT*.

The Golden Key and Other Fairy Tales, George MacDonald. New York: Eerdmans, 1950.

'Hansel and Gretel', in *CGFT*.

'Iron Hans', in *CGFT*.

'Jack and the Beanstalk', in *Fairy Tales*.

'Jonah' ('The Book of Jonah') in *The Old Testament*.

'Jorinda and Joringel', in *CGFT*.

'The Juniper Tree', in *CGFT*.

'King Thrushbeard', in *CGFT*.

'The King of the Golden Mountain', in *CGFT*.

The Light Princess, George MacDonald. New York: Eerdmans, 1980.

The Little Red Hen: An Old Story, Margot Zemach. New York: Farrar, Straus & Giroux, 1983.

'Little Snow White', in *CGFT*.

'Mother Holle', in *CGFT*.

'Our Lady's Child', in *CGFT*.

Peronnik: A French Tale of the Grail Quest, Emile Souvestre (illus.). Rochester, VT: Inner Traditions, 1984.

The Princess and Curdie, George MacDonald. New York: Eerdmans, 1987.

'Puss-in-Boots', in *Fairy Tales*.

'The Queen of the Bees', in *CGFT*.

'The Quest of the Golden Fleece', in *Mythology*, Edith Hamilton. Boston: Little, Brown, 1942.

'Rapunzel', in *CGFT*.

'Rip Van Winkle', Washington Irving. New York: Penguin, 1987.

'Rumplestiltskin', in *CGFT*.

'Saint George and the Dragon', adapted by Margaret Hodges. Boston: Little, Brown, 1984.

'The Seven Ravens', in *CGFT*.

'Snow White' ('Little Snow White'), in *CGFT*.

'The Singing, Soaring Lark', in *CGFT*.

'The Three Languages', in *CGFT*.

'Thornrose' ('Briar Rose', 'Sleeping Beauty') in *CGFT*.

'The Twelve Brothers', in *CGFT*.

'The Two Brothers', in *CGFT*.

'Vasilissa the Beautiful', in *Russian Folktales*. Robert Chandler (trans.). Boston: Shambhala/Random, 1980.

'The Wishing Table, the Donkey and the Stick', in *CGFT*.

'The Wolf and the Seven Little Kids', in *CGFT*.

Also recommended to deepen your story imagination are:

Cook, Elizabeth. 1969. *The Ordinary and the Fabulous*. Cambridge: Cambridge University Press.

Chinen, Allen B. 2002. *In the Everafter: Fairytales and the Second Half of Life*. Wilmette, IL: Chiron Publications.

– 1993. *Once Upon a Midlife: Classic Stories and Mythic Tales to Illuminate the Middle Years*. Los Angeles: Tarcher.

– 1997. *Beyond the Hero: Classic Stories of Men in Search of Soul*. xlibris.

– 1997. *Waking the World; Classic Tales of the Heroic Feminine*. Los Angeles: Tarcher.

Estes, Clarissa Pinkola. 1992. *Women Who Run with Wolves: Myths and Stories of the Wild Woman Archetype*. New York: Ballantine Books.

Gersie, Alida. 1990. *Storymaking in Education and Therapy*. London: Jessica Kingsley.

Keable, Georgiana, 2017. *The Natural Storyteller, Wildlife Tales for Telling*. Stroud, Gloucestershire, UK: Hawthorn Press.

– 1991. *Storymaking in Bereavement*. London: Jessica Kingsley.

– 1992. *Earthtales: Storytelling in Times of Change*. London: Merlin Press.

Hillman, James. 1975. *Re-visioning Psychology*. New York: Harper & Row.

Hollingsworth, Sue and Ramsden, Ashley, 2013. *The Storytellers Way: Sourcebook for inspired storytelling*. Stroud, Gloucestershire, UK: Hawthorn Press.

Johnston, Anita. 1996. *Eating by the Light of the Moon*. Carlsbad, CA: Gurze Books.

Jung, Carl. 1958. *Psyche and Symbol*. Garden City: Doubleday Anchor.

MacDonald, George. 1999. *Collected Fairy Tales*. London: Penguin.
– 1996 reissued edition. *The Princess and Curdie*. London: Puffin Classics.

Martin, Rafe. 1999. *The Hungry Tigress: Buddhist Myths, Legends & Jataka Tales*. Cambridge, MA: Yellow Moon Press.

Matthews, Paul. 2015. *Sing Me the Creation: Creative Writing Sourcebook*. Stroud, Gloucestershire, UK: Hawthorn Press.

Mellon, Nancy. 2000. *Storytelling with Children*. Stroud, Gloucestershire: Hawthorn Press.

Mellon, Nancy and Ramsden, Ashley. 2008. *Body Eloquence*. Santa Rosa, CA: Energy Psychology Press.

Meyer, Rudolf. 1988. *The Wisdom of Fairy Tales*. Edinburgh: Floris Books.

Pearson, Jenny. 1996. *Discovering the Self through Drama and Movement: The Sesame Approach*. London: Jessica Kingsley.

Pearson, Jenny et al. 2013. *Dramatherapy with Myth and Fairytale: The Golden Stories of Sesame*. London: Jessica Kingsley.

Perrow, Susan. 2008. *Healing Stories for Challenging Behaviour*. Stroud: Hawthorn Press.

Reman, Naomi Remen, M.D. 1994. *Kitchen Table Wisdom*. New York: Riverhead Books.

Shedlock, Marie L. 1951. *The Art of the Storyteller*. New York: Dover Publications.

Simpkinson, Charles and Anne, Editors. 1993. *Sacred Stories: A Celebration of the Power of Story to Transform and Heal*. San Francisco: Harper.

Thompson, Stith. 1978. *The Folktale*. University of California Press; Reprint Edition.

Von Frans, Marie Louise. 1972. *The Feminine in Fairy Tales*. Dallas: Spring Publications.

– 1977. *Individuation in Fairy Tales*. Dallas: Spring Publications.

– 1970. *Interpretation of Fairy Tales*. Dallas: Spring Publications.

Wyatt, Isabel. 2012, third edition. *The Seven-Year-Old Wonder Book*. Edinburgh: Floris.

– 2013, third edition. *Magical Wonder Tales: King Beetle Tamer and Other Stories*. Edinburgh: Floris.

Zipes, Jack. 1995. *Creative Storytelling: Building Community/Changing Lives*. London, UK: Routledge.

– 2000. *The Great Fairy Tale Tradition*. W. W. Norton Co.

– 2014. *The Complete Fairy Tales of the Brothers Grimm*. Princeton University Press.

– 2015. *The Oxford Companion to Fairy Tales*. Oxford University Press.

Afterword

A global renaissance of storytelling began in the early 1980s. Many felt called to strengthen heart and soul to give voice to personal and traditional tales as an antidote to the swiftly expanding television and computer industries. With feet planted, gestures alive, storytellers rose up with fully embodied voices, sometimes greatly surprised and fascinated to be identifying themselves in this way. Throughout the world, many storytellers banded together in living rooms, churches and cafes with warm enthusiasm and a growing sense of mission and cultural-artistic purpose. Eventually, story concerts and festivals were attracting eager crowds from all walks of life. Instead of distancing screened communications, they were hungry for authentic person-to-person sharing.

My own sense of language opened gradually. I empathize with all those whose listening and expression are asleep, or shy, or stunned. Though I was largely silent during my teen years I began to listen intuitively and musically. After several years of studying and teaching magnificent poetry, prose, drama, and exploring music and creative writing, I discovered Waldorf education. I was thrilled and fascinated to learn that all the teachers in Waldorf school present a global curriculum orally every day in the classroom. As I took up teaching by this method in my mid-thirties and expanded my soul and storytelling abilities, I was ever-inspired by the children's needs and their enthusiasm for stories. Over the years, as I practiced teaching through storytelling, integrated with painting, drawing and other child-centred activities, I also began to create stories to alleviate challenging adult and family situations. Gradually I discovered how imaginative stories can not only edify, and greatly nourish well-being, but also transform distress on many levels. I felt profoundly inspired to write this book to help bring forth the storyteller within every person. As the global storytelling movement expanded, parents and others who wanted to become storytellers called for the workshops and courses that I continue giving to this day. Many of their wonderful stories of personal transformation are included in this new edition.

In 1992 when this book was first published by Element Books and I was completing a training in Psychotherapy through the Arts, I met Ashley Ramsden, who was touring the USA with his astonishing storytelling performances. He was in the process of founding the School of Storytelling at Emerson College in Sussex, UK, which continues to this day to nourish aspiring and accomplished storytellers from around the world. I taught 'storytelling as a healing art' courses and workshops there until 2010 and helped Ashley to organize a decade of storytelling symposia on many themes.

Today I continue to maintain a private practice, and to explore how imagination, word-play, and creative expression of all sorts can serve well-being. As I travel near and far to teach the imaginative healing art of storytelling, amidst the depersonalizing aspects of electronic communications, I feel even more dedicated to the heart-warming mission of this book.

Nancy Mellon
www.healingstory.com

Other Books by Hawthorn Press

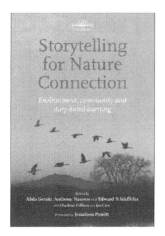

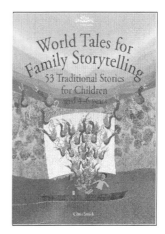

Ordering Books

If you have difficulties ordering Hawthorn Press
books from a bookshop, you can order direct from
our website, www.hawthornpress.com, or from our
UK distributor, BookSource: 50 Cambuslang Road,
Glasgow, G32 8NB: Tel: (0845) 370 0063, E-mail:
orders@booksource.net.

Details of our overseas distributors can be found on
our website.

Hawthorn Press

www.hawthornpress.com